AFTER THE PURIFYING

Paul G. Bretscher

Thirty-second Yearbook
Lutheran Education Association
7400 Augusta Street
River Forest, Illinois

Art Work

Del Klaustermeier
Walther Lutheran High School
Melrose Park, Illinois

TO THE MEMORY OF MY FATHER
PAUL M. BRETSCHER
EDUCATOR

AND OF MY MOTHER
MINNIE SPOHN BRETSCHER
HIS HELPER

Preface

When one attempts to assess the future of Lutheran education in the Missouri Synod, several cautions must be kept in mind. Educational assessments can be made on several different levels: academic, sociological, philosophical, theological, etc. What is found to be true on one level of investigation is not necessarily true for levels quite different in context. And what is true in general does not necessarily apply in specific situations. General assessments frequently give some direction in identifying central tendencies or areas of emphasis, but they do not answer the critical questions of purpose and necessity in particular cases.

Comparative studies now available provide ample evidence to warrant the conclusion that Lutheran schools are doing as well as, and in a significant number of instances better than, contemporaries in the public sector who operate in similar social, economic, and geographic contexts. There is no evidence known to me that a change will occur in this performance record in the near future for Lutheran schools. It is reasonable to expect that continued improvement in teaching and learning will be made in Lutheran as well as public education in response to heavy demands imposed upon them by a rapidly changing technological culture. However, academic achievement is not the crucial issue involved in the assessment proposed in this book.

A valid assessment of Lutheran education must deal specifically with the theological stance it espouses. Lutheran education is built on a religious base. The curriculum, the teaching acts, the learning process, and the grounds by which subject content is defined, utilized, and evaluated have a theological root. It is incongruous to think of Lutheran education in terms outside of a theological context. This does not mean that the so-called secular learnings and understandings available to us are not to be examined and explicated with considerable care and interest by teachers and students. Quite the contrary! In many respects Lutheran education is no different from any other kind of good education. The distinguishing characteristic between a Lutheran orientation to education and the approach found in

iv

the public sector is the *ground* (base) on which the educational enterprise is pursued. All learnings, insights, understandings, knowledge, skills, etc., are of God and they acquire their true meaning and perspective through a relationship to God. There certainly is no such thing as a Lutheran mathematics, biology, language arts, physical training, science, etc., but there certainly is a reality of God's making that determines the ground for our pursuit of these disciplines. A valid assessment of Lutheran education must include a critical examination of the rationale by which the entire educational enterprise is justified.

Lutheran education is pursued by a divine command to teach the faith in Christ Jesus in all its truth and purity. This is done in many ways in the home, church, school, and community. The means used to carry out this command are many and varied, and they are determined largely by tradition and the context in which the enterprise is carried out. This diversity of means is necessary and reasonable. Uniformity here is not necessarily a virtue. However, there is a uniformity demanded that distinguishes Lutheran from all other forms of instruction. This unity is to be found in fidelity to the "Word of God" and the administration of the Sacraments; fidelity not to a Book, a tradition, a legislative authority, or an elected leader, but unreservedly to the "Word of God." It is suggested that when this unifying factor is absent or diluted with a plus, then the educational enterprise is not truly Lutheran.

So we come to the root question in our assessment of the future of Lutheran education, namely, "Is Lutheran education faithful to the teaching of the faith in Christ Jesus as that faith is known through the Word of God?" To answer this crucial question, Lutheran education must make it crystal clear what it means by the "Word of God." The answer to that question is the burden of this book. Unless and until this root question is answered in conformity with the Scriptures, without equivocation or concession to tradition, the future of Lutheran education will be bleak indeed. Those who teach need to orient themselves to a foundation that is purified of the dross of ambiguity that has plagued us so long and has recently caused disastrous differences among us.

The L.E.A. offers this book as a significant contribution to Lutheran educational thought. The material presented in this book presumes no finality but it offers instead a serious invitation to search, to pray, and to dialogue dispassionately for a Scripturally sound and God pleasing consensus concerning the teaching function of the Church. The Association recognizes that diversity of choice among viable options is a necessary condition in the democratic process of reaching a consensus, and that change in thought and practice is usually born in controversy. To disagree gracefully in love for the brother as one reaches for the truth is an essential element of discipleship.

The author has provided a lucid and provocative book that is pleasantly devoid of much academic jargon. He has also included an abundance of documentation as chapter-end notes to help the reader search out the evidence needed to make his own assessment and to develop his own solution to the critical question, "What is the Word of God?" On the answer to that question hinges the future of Lutheran education.

Paul W. Lange, Chairman
L.E.A. Editorial Committee

Table of Contents

Acknowledgments

When the Lutheran Education Association first proposed that I write its 1975 Yearbook, I saw more than merely an honor in the invitation. It opened to me an unexpected opportunity to assemble and focus for the church a wide range of insights and concerns for Lutheran education which had been growing in me over many years. I took it to be the Lord's hand.

In the months that followed, His grace was evident repeatedly. A major sign of it was the continuing support and trust I experienced from the L.E.A. Board as such and, more directly, from members of the editorial committee who read my developing manuscript along the way. Their cautions, critiques, and insights were always stimulating and enriching—a visible illustration of how the Body of Christ grows by and needs the variety of gifts the Spirit invests in its members. I think in particular of Paul W. Lange, Alice Peppler, Carl Halter, Douglas Mosel, and J. D. Weinhold. To that list I must add also Dorothy Lange, who joined her husband, Paul, in investing uncounted hours of her own talent, zeal, and love in the project. Others also have contributed their gifts—Delmar Klaustermeier, his artistic imagination and skills; Stephen Schmidt, his talent for management and distribution; Henry Simon, his promoting; and Dorothy Czamanske, her typing.

In the background stands our entire church. This book draws on what I have absorbed and cannot begin to credit from conversations without number—sometimes private, sometimes around a table, sometimes in committees or conferences. What it has become can be explained only in terms of a long process of reading, listening, feeling, absorbing, testing by the rule and norm of Scripture, assimilating, integrating, trying to make sense out of things, and finally returning the outcome to the church for its own study and further testing. I can only be grateful, therefore, to all who have laid themselves open to criticism by saying out loud what they were thinking and feeling in terms of what made sense to them. This, too, is surely from the hand of God.

There remains to be mentioned the patience of my wife, Marguerite, and our children, and the continuing trust and support of Immanuel congregation of which I am a Pastor. For these gifts, too, I can only thank God.

Now we must release what has emerged. It is the best that I and those who worked with me can offer at this time. Our desire has been to magnify the glory of Christ and the Gospel for which the L.E.A. itself has stood throughout its thirty-three years. We therefore implore the Lord's blessings on this book, and count on His grace to cover its deficiencies. May He use it toward realizing not our frail purposes, but His own gracious will toward the church He loves and has bought with His own blood.

Paul G. Bretscher
Valparaiso, Indiana
Epiphany, 1975

Prologue

The conflict which has been tearing The Lutheran Church—Missouri Synod for the past several years has overwhelming significance for the future of education in our church.

The first focus of that conflict was, after all, an educational institution, Concordia Seminary in St. Louis. So intense has the conflict been, that it has yielded two seminaries, one a "Concordia Seminary in Exile" (Seminex), the other a restructured Concordia at the old address. Which of these, if either, is the "real" Concordia Seminary? That question is more than political and constitutional. It involves conflicting understandings of the Word of God, of the church, and thus of Christian education.

The St. Louis Seminary is only the most visible frontier of the conflict. The Synod's entire educational system is involved, including Concordia Theological Seminary in Springfield; Concordia teachers colleges at River Forest, Seward, and St. Paul; Concordia Senior College at Fort Wayne; and ten preparatory schools. After that the tension affects also Lutheran high schools, day schools, Sunday schools, Bible classes, and every developed or developing agency of teaching on the parish level. The nature of future educational materials, the gifts of persons whom the church calls upon to develop such materials, Concordia Publishing House which prints such materials, all are deeply affected. Ultimately, the dispute has to do with our children and how they are taught. Thereby it reaches into every home.

It might seem prudent, at first glance, for the Lutheran Education Association to avoid the issue, stay out of the heat and the pain, and limit its concerns to relatively safe frontiers which do not strike so dangerously close to the heart. The more realistic course is to face the challenge openly and with evangelical candor. Never in our history, perhaps, has it been so necessary to involve the entire Synod in the task of re-examining what Lutheran education is and ought to be, and to test the most basic assumptions of our past tradition and practice.

It is not expedient to delegate this task to committees of "experts." Whoever the experts may be, they are personally caught in the struggle just as deeply as any of us. We are not dealing here with outcomes of Lutheran education such as sociologists purport to measure. We are dealing with what goes into our teaching, that is, with the Word of God in Lutheran education. That question touches Christianity itself at its very heart.

We can face the issue without fear, so long as we set our hope in our Lord Jesus Christ and not in our own reason and strength, or wisdom and rightness. With eyes on the cross, following Him who is the Way, we can walk His path even under the strain of our differences. In Christ we can cling to one another, honor the gifts which the Spirit has invested in each of us, and gladly be changed more fully into the image of Him who is also our Truth and our Life.

This Yearbook offers to members of the Lutheran Education Association, and to the church, not an end to the discussion that is so necessary, but a beginning.

Chapter I

The Purifying

EXPERIENCING THE FIRE

Our title embodies a vision. It suggests that what is happening in the Missouri Synod now is a purifying. A dross is being purged away. When the Lord's work of refining is finished, a purity that had been marred will be restored. But what will our church look like then? What impurities will have been separated out and left behind? Obviously, a process of purifying means that changes have occurred. How will Lutheran education have changed from what it was before? To search out such questions is more than a disturbing necessity. It is a great and unique opportunity, to which the Lord Himself is calling us.

The Concept of Purifying

The imagery of purifying is Biblical. We find it helpful and comforting to recall some key texts. A classic one from the history of the destruction of Jerusalem and the exile of Judah is Ezekiel 22: 17-22.[1]

> And the Word of the Lord came to me: "Son of man, the house of Israel has become dross to me; all of them, silver and bronze and tin and lead in the furnace, have become dross. Therefore thus says the Lord God: Because you have all become dross, therefore, behold, I will gather you into the midst of Jerusalem. As men gather silver and bronze and iron and lead and tin into a furnace, to blow the fire upon it in order to melt it; so I will gather you in my anger and in my wrath, and I will put you in and melt you. I will gather you and blow upon you with the fire of my wrath, and you shall be melted in the midst of it. As silver is melted in a furnace, so you shall be melted in the midst of it; and you shall know that I the Lord have poured out my wrath upon you."

Behind the evident pain and fury of the Babylonian invasion stood the purposeful wrath of God, melting His people, purifying them so that they might again know, trust, and serve Him.

The theme recurs by way of promise in Malachi 3:1-4. God's people yearn for His coming. They will delight in the messenger who

3

prepares His way. But they do not realize what His coming will do to them.

> Who can stand when he appears? For he is like a refiner's fire . . . and he will purify the sons of Levi and refine them like gold and silver, till they present right offerings to the Lord.

Although the priestly sons of Levi think they are serving the Lord faithfully, they fail to see their own dross. That is why the Lord's coming will be so painful and frightening to them. Nevertheless the very fire testifies how precious they are, like gold and silver, in God's sight.

The promise of cleansing was "filled full" in the history of John the Baptist and of Jesus. The messenger of the Lord called on the people of Israel to repent and thus to let go of their dross. Baptism offered instant cleansing and restoration to God. Jesus signaled the purifying when He cleansed lepers and drove out unclean spirits. Ultimately, however, the purifying had to penetrate to people's hearts. "Blessed are the pure in heart," Jesus said (Matt. 5:8). The kind of purifying the Pharisees performed under the Law would not suffice.

> Woe to you, . . . for you cleanse the outside of the cup and of the plate, but inside they are full of extortion and rapacity. You blind Pharisee! First cleanse the inside of the cup and of the plate, that the outside also may be clean (Matt. 23:25-26).

The day we call Good Friday exposed the dross in full. No gold was to be found in Pilate and the Gentiles, in Caiaphas and the Jews, in the disciples, or in us. The only gold was Jesus Himself. At that moment, however, God's miracle of love turned everything around. The refining fire consumed Jesus instead of the world of sinners. In love for us and for His Father, Jesus was willing to have it so.[2] That is why 1 John 1:7 attaches our purifying so vividly to the blood, "the blood of Jesus his Son cleanses us from all sin," and to the water of baptism with the blood.[3] To proclaim the continuing wonder of that purifying is the very glory of Lutheran education, and its power.

If the fire that threatens to consume our church today is truly from the Lord, we need not fear its pain. Our God surely knows what the dross is from which we must be cleansed. In His own way and time, and through whatever instruments He chooses, He will make that clear to us, and thus cleanse us also of every inadequate and mis-

4

taken diagnosis. He asks only that we trust Him and search His Word together and without fear, praying earnestly to understand what is happening to us. That kind of searching does not belong to pastors only, but to teachers and laymen as well. Indeed, teachers have a very special stake in the Lord's purifying. Whatever separating of gold from dross may occur, it impinges immediately on Lutheran education, that is, on the Word of God which we teach and the way we teach it.

Every question, ambiguity, or nagging inadequacy which has tormented Lutheran educators in the past belongs to the struggle. We shall pose some of our own questions here, not in the expectation of being able to answer them all, but to stimulate at least an awareness of how serious the matters are which lie before us.

There is the obvious first question: How do we teach religion? And why should we expect our people to believe and continue to believe what we teach, in the face of the sophisticated secularism of our time?

Why do many of our youth drift away? Why do many come to regard the Word as irrelevant, and to look upon the church as a religious institution without meaning for them?

Why do some who were brought up in our educational system experience what they call "real hell" as they try to hang on to what they are taught? Why do some preserve Christianity for themselves only by discarding or restructuring certain things they learned? Why do others discover sanity and freedom only by renouncing what they had been taught to believe?

Is the truth and purity of God's Word fixed in a body of doctrine to be taught? Or is our structure of doctrine itself subject to continual purging and renewal through whatever testings the Lord may choose to lay upon any or all of His people?

How can it happen that in our conflict what one party calls "freedom in the Gospel" the other attacks as "permissiveness"? And what do these drastically conflicting opinions imply for the very process and impact of education in the church?

Does our structure of education yield a sense of denominational rightness? Does it become a standard by which we judge the wrongness of others? Does it thereby erect and perpetuate walls within Christendom rather than break them down?

Is our foundation of truth in Christ sufficiently firm that we may enjoy the variety of gifts which the Spirit invests in the Body rather than fear them as a threat? Is our unity in Christ sufficient to hold in love those among us who may be wrong as well as those who are right? Does our foundation set us free to discover that we ourselves have been wrong, and yet not be shattered by such a discovery?

How does Lutheran education inculcate a wholesome relationship for the Christian to that which is secular? What does it mean for a Christian to live freely and responsibly in God's created world and within a fallen humanity God has not abandoned, yet without compromising his character as God's saint in Christ?

What is the proper use of the mind? How shall Lutheran education encourage people to think? When is thinking and questioning a proper use of God-given reason to be exercised in all courage, obedience, and freedom? On the other hand, what kind of thinking is properly depicted as "rationalism"? Only as that distinction becomes clear can Lutheran education challenge intellects and set them free to serve God in Biblical study, preaching, and witnessing.

What is conscience? What is involved when people appeal to their conscience? What does it mean for a conscience to be captive to the Word of God and, in that very captivity, to be free? How shall Lutheran education encourage a joyful and courageous freedom of conscience which can also honor the consciences of brothers even in situations of disagreement and conflict?

To face questions such as these with all seriousness is already to enter the fire.

The Purifying of Missouri

The refining fire rages within the Missouri Synod, consuming, dividing, threatening to shatter us. It has broken through into congregations and families. It refuses to be contained behind lines of structured authority. It will not leave teachers and laity undisturbed. To the hearts of many an individual saint the fire is utterly dismaying and incomprehensible. It appears to be political, of men, and indeed it is. Yet without contradiction the fire is from the Lord. That is our comfort. Our God must truly love us, to devote so much attention to us. There is a dross to be purged out of us. Somehow, His grace considers us worth the effort. In His sight we too are still silver and gold.

The New Orleans Convention of The Lutheran Church—Missouri Synod was heralded as "a doctrinal crossroads." [4] A dross needed to be purged out so that the Synod might be restored to full doctrinal purity. As the majority of delegates understood the issue, a view of Scripture had entered the church, through the use of the "histori-cal-critical method" of interpretation, which put the Scriptures at the mercy of man's reason. It seemed impossible that men who approved that method could any longer "accept without reservation" the Scriptures as the Word of God (Synod's Constitution, Article II), inspired and inerrant. The inevitable effect of the method, it seemed, would be to erode the authority of the Scriptures and to undermine the Gospel. Theologians who claimed to derive the authority of the Scriptures from the authority of the Gospel were suspected of "Gospel reductionism," and of trying to change the doctrinal basis on which the Synod had stood for 125 years.[5]

The Convention felt constrained to restate the Synod's doctrinal position against current antitheses by adopting "A Statement of Scriptural and Confessional Principles." [6] It also adopted a resolution associating false doctrine with the position of the faculty majority at Concordia Seminary, St. Louis.[7] It recorded charges of false doctrine as well as of malfeasance against the President of that seminary.[8] The Convention acted on the conviction that the dross from which the church must be purified was concentrated most acutely at the St. Louis seminary. From there its poisons were spreading into the whole church. If the dross which originated at the seminary could be purged, then in time the whole church would be cleansed.

The Convention also resolved

> That the Synod understand Article II of its Constitution as permitting, and at times even requiring, the formulation and adoption of doctrinal statements as definitive of the Synod's position relative to controverted issues.[9]

It declared that such statements

> insofar as they are in accord with the Scriptures and the pattern of doctrine set forth in the Lutheran Symbols, are . . . binding upon all its members.[10]

We may notice here an unresolved difficulty. The Convention adopted "A Statement of Scriptural and Confessional Principles" by a vote of 55 per cent. No doubt the majority felt that this doctrinal statement was indeed "in accord with the Scriptures and the pattern of doctrine set forth in the Lutheran Symbols." But if the 45 per cent who voted otherwise were persuaded that "A Statement" was *not* "in accord with the Scriptures" and the pattern of sound Confessional doctrine, how could a mere Convention vote change their minds? [11]

Nevertheless, the purifying had been set in motion. The Convention elected to various boards and committees men it could trust to see the purging through. Conformity to the Synod's rulings was expected on the part of all members. The Synod had spoken and its members, for the sake of their "walking together" as a "syn-od," were to listen. Any who did not submit had the appearance of insurgents against duly constituted authority, rebels against the Word of God, defenders of the dross. Thus when Evangelical Lutherans in Mission (ELIM) was founded as a "confessing movement within Synod" in August, 1973, it was viewed as a divisive force.

The purifying fire continued to rage. In January, 1974, the Board of Control of Concordia Seminary, St. Louis, suspended the Seminary's President.

The majority of the faculty responded by declaring that they too were suspended by the Board's action, since whatever charges were lodged against their President must hold also against them. Their call for defined charges and their appeal to the Word of God and to conscience gained no hearing. Since they were not doing their work, but were seemingly in defiance of the Synod which employed them, their jobs were terminated and their homes and offices ordered vacated. The result was the founding of "Concordia Seminary in Exile" or "Seminex." That led in turn to a crisis concerning the placement of Seminex graduates and their ordination, without certification by Synod's authorized seminary at the 801 DeMun address. Congregations, districts, and district presidents who participated in such calling and ordaining were declared in violation of Synod's *Handbook* and subject to discipline and expulsion.[12]

Painful as all such conflicts were, the synodical administration did not waver in its determination to carry out the mandate of the New Orleans Convention, namely, to purify the Synod of its dross. Once the corrective measures were accomplished, it was felt, the purified church would again bring to God offerings "pleasing to the

Lord as in the days of old and as in former years" (Malachi 3:4).

It should be possible, therefore, for someone to write a book under our title, *After the Purifying,* and to elaborate on the implications of the purifying for Lutheran education in the Missouri Synod from the perspective of the Convention majority. Imagine the day when the fire ceases, the cleansing is finished, and all is at peace. What will Christian education be like then? What kind of church, teachers, instructional materials, families, and children do we look for in this ideal and visionary future? In this book we shall have our eye on just such questions. Everything depends, however, on what the Lord's fire is really doing. What is the dross which He is determined to separate out from the gold? If the dross turns out to be something other than what the Synod's 1973 Convention assumed it to be, the implications of the purifying for Lutheran education will also be very different.

We must therefore pursue the gold, that is, the truth in Christ which alone can unify. If two visions conflict, they cannot have equal legitimacy. It will not do to retreat to Pilate's despairing skepticism, "What is truth?" as though there were no answer. Neither dare we escape into pluralism, or into mutterings about "another side to it." Somewhere, sometime, at whatever risk of change and shattering, the issue must be met. Now, in the heat of the fire, is the Lord's time.

Purifying as the Work of God

In its pursuit of purity, the New Orleans Convention was convinced that it was doing the work of God. Indeed, it was. We have suggested that the dross to be separated out from the gold may be something quite different from what the Convention imagined. Nevertheless it appears likely even from our very limited insight into this agonizing history, that the real dross might never have been exposed for what it is, had it not been for the fury and pain of our desperate human conflict.

The texts on purifying from Ezekiel and Malachi now become the more revealing. The church does not purify itself by its own reason and strength, diagnosis and prescription, organization and effort. The Lord Himself does the purifying. It is God who gathers His people into the fire, blows the flame to full fury, and melts them down as necessary so as to reveal the pure metal and consume the dross. For all their pain His people are to trust Him and let Him have His way with them. One day they will know fully what He has done and give Him all praise. Jeremiah 30:24 expresses the painful promise beautifully:

> The fierce anger of the Lord will not turn back until he has executed and accomplished the intents of his mind. In the latter days you will understand this.

When the church undertakes to purify itself, however, the record reveals one story after another of mistaken zeal, misuse of power, and persecution. For the church is blind to its own impurity! It always tends to treasure as gold what the Lord sees to be dross. Whatever is fixed by long tradition, the church hallows as sacred. Whatever exposes distortions in the tradition and calls for change (repentance), the church attacks as wrong. The church is readily distracted from the real enemy—sin, unbelief, flesh, and the deceits of the devil. It identifies as enemy any strange ideas which seem threatening and any people who express and persist in such ideas. These people are the "troublers of Israel." In the interest of "peace" and in defense of God's unchangeable "truth," they must be suppressed and silenced. The majority always finds security in the familiar, and counts on duly constituted leaders to deliver it from any threat. Therefore God's prophets are inevitably a minority, sometimes a minority of only one.

The record is clear and consistent. Elijah is persecuted by people who have forsaken the covenant of the Lord, yet will not know it.[13] Ahab relies on his 400 prophets and hates Micaiah.[14] Jeremiah is accused of unbelief and of undermining the people's faith in the Lord's promises to save and glorify Jerusalem.[15] Herod demonstrates by power that he does not have to listen to the disruptive voice of John the Baptist.[16] Caiaphas and the Council defend the purity of their religion by naming Jesus the sinner and blasphemer.[17] The Council commands Peter and John not to disturb the holy city by speaking in the name of Jesus and not to make them guilty of Jesus' blood.[18] Saul of Tarsus fights zealously to preserve the Old Covenant by persecuting the New.[19] Leo X excommunicates Luther. Always it is done in the name of "purifying," of holy tradition, of peace, of authority and responsibility for the welfare of the church, and of service to God.

10

Synod's Constitution anticipates the danger. Against any use of institutional majority or ecclesiastical authority to decide matters of doctrine and of conscience, it insists that such matters be decided "only by the Word of God," [20] that is, by Scripture properly used as the "only rule and norm." [21] When the Word of God is searched and permitted to speak, then the Spirit of Truth will in His time and through the varied gifts in Christ's Body, expose what the dross really is. It is the Spirit's work to "convince the world of sin and of righteousness and of judgment," for the Spirit knows "the ruler of this world" and will not be distracted by something less than the true enemy.[22] Christ Himself, whose Spirit this is, did not save the world by cutting off and getting rid of certain stubborn, unworthy, or heretical people. He chose rather to be cut off Himself, in love for His Father and for us all.

After the purifying, Luthern education will understand more clearly why the church cannot purify itself. The church presumes to know what the impurity is, yet is so easily mistaken! Jesus' own disciples had to make that shattering discovery. Only through the purifying disaster of Jesus' death did they come to know the dross of their enthusiasm to make Him a king. Only then were they able to understand the Scriptures as He taught them.[23] Without God's fire we do not know our own dross! We think of the dross as gold, indispensable, to be defended with all zeal and conscience!

The Pharisees provide a classic illustration. They thought they were gold, free of the old idolatries, blameless under the law. Measuring Jesus by their dross they pronounced Him the sinner, for He healed on the Sabbath, was careless of the kosher, and ate with sinners. Jesus tried to make the Pharisees see what they were doing. "For the sake of your tradition, you have made void the Word of God," He said (Matt. 15:6), but they could not understand. Therefore Jesus prayed for the fire:

> I came to cast fire upon the earth; and would that it were already kindled! I have a baptism to be baptized with; and how I am constrained until it is accomplished! Do you think that I have come to give peace on earth? No, I tell you, but rather division (Luke 12:49-51).

Saul of Tarsus is the classic example of a Pharisee cleansed by fire from the dross he had once defended as gold. He testified how all his old advantages under the law had become "refuse" and "loss" to him, because of "the surpassing worth of knowing Christ" (Phil. 3:7-8).

The Simplicity of Purity

The fire we are experiencing is not to be regretted. We yearn and pray only that it may have its proper effect, that we may emerge purified of what God sees our dross to be. The purity God intends for us turns out to be a very simple thing. His Word unfolds it ever so clearly. We have only one purity, namely, the purity won for us in the blood of Christ, conferred on us in baptism and grasped by faith. By Jesus' blood our conscience is purified "from dead works to serve the living God" (Heb. 9:14). *Christ alone, grace alone, faith alone,* by means of Word and Sacrament, that is the purity which Scripture proclaims, the purity of every saint, and the purity of the Church. When the Confessions speak of "the Gospel preached in its purity," they mean the Word of God offering sinners the purity of Christ alone. Anything added to this purity or any claim that this purity is somehow not enough belongs to the dross.

More than theological discussion is required for us to recognize the glory of our purity, however, and to see the dross that must be purged. We need the gift and miracle of the Spirit, the "enlightening" of our hearts, as Luther speaks of it in the Third Article of his Small Catechism. Read that article with care. The church does not "keep" itself and its members in the "one true faith" and in the "pure doctrine of the Gospel." This is the work of the Spirit. Our natural impulse in the flesh is to imagine that we, by virtue of our organization as a Synod, have the power to possess pure doctrine, formulate it in documents, inculcate it in our schools, keep it pure, and even enforce it by discipline. That very notion is already dross! Yet so powerful is its hold on us that only the heat of God's smelting fire, threatening to consume faith and church, Bible and Gospel, ourselves and everything we have cherished, can free us of it!

DETECTING THE DROSS

At its roots our dross involves a subtle and pervasive confusion regarding "the Word of God." For four and a half centuries Lutheranism has focused its educational materials and processes upon the Word of God. The classic "first" among such materials is Luther's

Small Catechism or "Christliche Lehre," as he refers to it in his preface. The Catechism was to be an instrument for teaching the Word of God in homes and schools, so that those so taught might believe the Word and live by it.

"The Word of God" in Luther's Catechism

Recall the abundant references to the Word in Luther's Catechism.[25]

> Those who fear and love God will not despise His *Word* and the preaching of it, but deem it holy and gladly hear and learn it (Third Commandment).
>
> God's name is hallowed whenever His *Word* is taught clearly and purely, and we as His children lead holy lives in accordance with it (First Petition).
>
> His kingdom comes when by His Spirit and grace we believe His holy *Word* (Second Petition).
>
> His will is to keep us steadfast in His *Word* and faith, against all enemies (devil, world, flesh) who would distract us from that *Word* (Third Petition).
>
> Baptism forgives sin, regenerates in the Holy Spirit, justifies us through God's grace in Christ, makes us heirs of eternal life, buries us and raises us from the dead—not by water in itself, but through the *Word* and promise of God connected with that water, and through faith which relies on that *Word*.
>
> Our eating and drinking in the Sacrament of the Altar yields its benefits through the *words* "for you" and "for the forgiveness of sins." He who believes what these *words* say to him, is truly worthy and has what they promise.

At least twenty times the Catechism refers explicitly in this way to "the Word of God."

In his explanation of the Third Article (and here alone in the Small Catechism) Luther's term for the Word of God is "the Gospel."

> Through the Gospel the Holy Spirit has called, enlightened, sanctified, and preserved me, just as he gathers thereby the whole Christian church on earth in union with Jesus Christ in the one true faith. In this church the Spirit daily and abundantly speaks to me the Word of total forgiveness, promising thereby also to raise me from death and to grant eternal life to me and to all who (through that same Word) believe in Christ.

The Large Catechism shows how freely interchangeable the terms

13

"Gospel" and "Word of God" are in the mind of Luther. The Holy Spirit, Luther says,

> has a unique community in the world. It (this community) is the mother that begets and bears every Christian through *the Word of God*. The Holy Spirit reveals and preaches that *Word,* and by it he illumines and kindles hearts so that they grasp and accept it, cling to it and persevere in it. Where he does not cause the *Word* to be preached and does not awaken understanding in the heart, all is lost.[26]

Luther's concept of "the Word of God" is absolutely fundamental to any understanding and discussion of Lutheran education. Yet it is precisely over "the Word of God" that the deepest theological conflict rages in the Lutheran Church—Missouri Synod. The whole future of education in our church depends on our understanding of that term. Here above all else the purifying fire must separate gold from dross.

We must, therefore, examine closely the phrase "the Word of God" and put to the test our ideas concerning it. It is clear from the Catechisms that in Luther's mind "the Word of God" is not simply equivalent to the Bible. It stands rather for specific things that God is saying, which He expects us to believe in our hearts, concerning our relationship to Him. God's Word is that message by which the Spirit creates and gathers the Church, and which the Church in turn preaches and teaches, not only in pulpit and classroom, but also in absolution and the sacraments. The Word of God proclaims grace and forgiveness in Christ to the sinner. Its content is the wisdom and promises of God for sanctification and eternal life. This concept of "the Word of God" belongs to what the Confessions and Lutheran theology know as "the means of grace." [27]

"The Word of God" in Missouri's Tradition

In Missouri Synod tradition and piety, however, the term "the Word of God" is dominated by quite another meaning, though we have never quite realized or defined the difference. According to this "Missouri" meaning, the Word of God is simply equated with the Holy Scriptures. Scripture is understood to be the Word of God, not by and for the sake of the Gospel, but in its formal totality as a Book. Indeed, when some brethren insist that Scripture is the Word of God according to the "means of grace" (Gospel) understanding of that term, without implying the totality of the Bible as Book, they are charged with "Gospel Reductionism." In the Synod's tradition and piety, Scripture is the Word of God according to a meaning derived from the doctrine of inspiration and certified by Missouri's understanding of the sentence fragment, "All Scripture is given by inspiration of God" (2 Tim. 3:16). Thus the term "the Word of God" stands for the inspired canon of sixty-six books.

From this "inspiration" concept of the Word of God, certain inferences proceed quite logically. "God is therefore the true Author of every word of Scripture," that is, of the Book.[28] It follows that Scripture as canonical book possesses qualities appropriate to its divine authorship: holiness, spirit, power, authority, inerrancy, clarity, uniqueness. It follows also that anyone who makes distinctions or raises questions of a historical or literary nature in Bible study has the appearance of a "Bible doubter." [29] He is suspected of undermining and attacking "the Word of God," of not submitting to God but rebelling against Him. For Scripture as Book is synonymous with "the Word of God." The Bible is therefore to be believed in everything it says, without wavering. Indeed, to believe the Bible from cover to cover in simple, child-like faith, questioning nothing, has become for many the very definition of "evangelical" Christianity over against "liberalism."

We of the Missouri Synod have been using the same term, "the Word of God," in two very different meanings, without knowing it, without distinguishing, and without analyzing. What are the consequences of this ambiguity?

Consequences in Logical and Theological Thinking

First, on the level of clear and logical discourse, the consequence is bound to be confusion, misunderstanding, suspicion, and a thwarting of intelligible conversation.

For example, Article II of the Synod's Constitution declares that the Synod and every member "accepts without reservation" the Scriptures "as the written Word of God." But what do the members of the Synod have in mind when they hear and use that phrase, "the Word of God"? To many, perhaps most, it means the inspired and inerrant Scriptures, with God as the true Author of every word.

15

To a minority, however, "the Word of God" means the Spirit's proclamation of grace in Christ to sinners, and the Scriptures as the fountain and norm of that Word. Since neither side has noticed or defined the ambiguity, much less resolved it, conversation is thwarted before it even begins. Indeed, in the eyes of the majority, their brethren are equivocating, misleading the church, and trying to change the Synod's doctrine, when they claim to accept Scripture as the Word of God "without reservation" according to Article II.

The confusion is endless. To submit to Scripture as "the Word of God" by the "Gospel" meaning of that phrase is quite different from submitting to Scripture's authority by way of the doctrine of inspiration. "Faith" or "child-like faith" in God by way of His Gospel promises is quite different from "faith" in the inspired and inerrant Bible. When the Confessions are read with the "Gospel" understanding of the term "the Word of God" and of "Scripture," they communicate something quite different from what comes through to anyone who reads them with the "inspiration" understanding. The fact that the Confessions do not explicitly distinguish between the two meanings we are detecting now in the term "the Word of God" (it was not an issue for them), belongs to the long background of our current difficulties.[30]

Second, not only logical, but also theological questions are involved in the ambiguity of the term "the Word of God." For example, we declare in Article II of our Constitution that Scripture "as the written Word of God" is our "only rule and norm of faith and practice." Article VIII,C confirms this when it states, "All matters of doctrine and of conscience shall be decided only by the Word of God." But what does "the Word of God" mean in our Constitution and in the Lutheran Confessions? If that term has the Gospel meaning we detected in Luther's Catechisms, then the Confessions make clear and consistent sense whenever they distinguish the Gospel from Scripture. For example, our confessing fathers declare that the Gospel, centering in justification by faith alone,

> is of special service for the clear, correct understanding of the entire Holy Scriptures, and alone shows the way to the unspeakable treasure and right knowledge of Christ, and alone opens the door to the entire Bible.[31]

In the Confessions, it would seem, Scripture understood through the

Gospel is our "only rule and norm." Thus "faith and practice" has to do with the knowledge of God and the life we live in relation to Him through the Spirit.

But if "the Word of God" in Article II means "the inspired and inerrant Scripture," we find ourselves in a different world of theological thought. In that case we have in mind the Bible, with God as the true Author of every word. Our concept of plenary divine authorship immediately reduces the Gospel to only a "part" of the Bible. The Bible is now *larger* than the Gospel. The Word of God is not only the Gospel and its articles, but also the rest of the Bible. Christians must "accept matters taught in the Scriptures that are not a part of the 'Gospel.' " [32] for "the Synod accepts anything and everything that the Scriptures teach." [33] In that case "the door to the entire Bible" does not have to be opened by first understanding the Gospel. On the contrary "the clear meaning of the canonical text" [34] will be readily perceptible to all who simply accept without reservation the Bible as the Word of God. Given that presupposition, they will surely agree on what the clear or "evident meaning of the Biblical text" is.[35] Such agreement, quite apart from agreeing in Christ and the Gospel, belongs to the true unity of the church and to our "walking together" as a Synod.[36]

From this understanding of "the Word of God" in Article II of the Constitution, it follows logically that the Synod has the "right" to "promote unity and resist individualism" by speaking "definitively to current issues." [37] As for the terms "faith and practice" in Article II, "faith" now has to do with holding faithfully to the doctrine of inspiration and inerrancy of the Bible apart from and larger in scope than the Gospel.[38] "Practice," in turn, has to do not only with a life of faith, hope, and love through Christ our Lord, but in particular now with methods and exegetical persuasions in Biblical study.

Consequences in Lutheran Education

Our long ambiguity and unsuspected double meaning with regard to the term "the Word of God" has resulted not only in logical confusions which have utterly thwarted meaningful discussion, and not only in theological division which is driving us toward schism, but also in severe handicaps to Lutheran education. Our ultimate concern in this book has to be with the damaging consequences such ambiguity can have on the faith and life of all who are affected by our teaching.

We celebrate the Word of God in our hymnody. We sing,

> God's Word is our great heritage
> And shall be ours forever;
> To spread its light from age to age
> Shall be our chief endeavor.
> Through life it guides our way
> In death it is our stay.
> Lord, grant, while world endure,
> We keep its teachings pure
> Throughout all generations.[39]

But what do we mean by "God's Word"? Unless we can answer that question unambiguously, we do not clearly know our own "great heritage." The Lord's purifying intends that we shall know what the "Word" is which we teach, and how to teach it. After the purifying "the Word of God" will have one meaning for us, and not two. If in the process of the purifying a dross is exposed and left behind, we shall not regret the loss, but only praise God for His rich grace.

This book could not be written unless we had already come to some judgment as to what the dross may be. The insights we share in the coming chapters do not derive from a willful individualism or pride of reason on our part. They derive from, and were forced upon us, by the experience of the fire. The fact that the fire is raging so widely through our whole church, piercing individual hearts with its pain and fear, gives hope that many will read with compassion and try to understand. It is most necessary, however, that the reader bring to bear all the gifts the Spirit has invested in him, so as to test our judgments by his own, his own by ours, and both his and ours by "Scripture . . . as the only rule and norm."

We shall unfold the thesis that the authentic meaning of the phrase "the Word of God" is that found in Luther's Catechisms. The Spirit speaks the Word of God's grace to our hearts out of the cross of Christ. By means of that Word He works the miracle of faith. The closest synonym for "the Word of God" is "the Gospel" in all its senses, including also the antithetical "Law." [40] We shall unfold its content extensively in the next chapter.

Wherever Scripture itself uses the term "the Word of God" or parallel expressions, the content of His Word is consistently God's communication of Law or Grace to the hearts of men. We honor Scripture as our "only rule and norm" when we take the trouble to examine its texts in order to see what the Scriptures themselves have in mind when they speak of "the Word." We honor the Confessions when we capture and make use of their insight that the Gospel of justification by faith alone is the key which opens to us the entire Holy Scriptures.

The Word of God, meaning Christ and the Gospel which proclaims Him, is the true glory and authority of the Bible. For the sake of that message it is proper to call the Holy Scriptures "the Word of God." Biblical texts ascribe to this Law-Gospel "Word of God" many precious qualities. They declare that God speaks the truth and does not lie,[41] that His Word is clear, a light to our path,[42] that His Word is powerful,[43] unique,[44] abiding,[45] alive and Spirited.[46]

But if these qualities are ascribed to the Scriptures simply as inspired Book, divinely authored, apart from and larger than the Word of God as Gospel, then they are misapplied. Indeed, a great robbery has occurred. For the glory which the Scriptures assign to Christ and the Gospel has then been misappropriated to the bare Bible. The consequences of such misappropriation are simply deadly. The Gospel as the Word of God is robbed of its honor. The power and authority of the Gospel is compromised and disparaged, for it is severed from and made to give way to another authority, namely, the "normative authority" which Scripture has by virtue of its inspiration.[47] As a result, the Gospel message comes to be regarded as a weak and feeble thing. No longer does the Word of the Gospel support us like an everlasting Rock.[48] On the contrary, the Gospel needs the doctrine of inspiration to support it,[49] and the authority of the church and its officials to support the doctrine of inspiration.[50] The glory and uniqueness of the Bible is no longer its message of life and salvation, but its inspiration.

It is not possible to pursue the problem of the dross further, however, until we have first re-examined the riches and comfort of the gold. We turn, therefore, to that Word of Spirit and Life which is Lutheran education's great treasure.

Footnotes for Chapter 1

[1] Unless otherwise indicated, the Scriptures are quoted in the Revised Standard Version.

[2] Luke 12:49; 22:42: John 13:1.

[3] 1 John 5:6.

[4] "President's Report," *Proceedings of the Fiftieth Regular Convention of The Lutheran Church—Missouri Synod,* New Orleans, Louisiana, July 6-13, 1973, p. 62.

[5] *Ibid.* For a rather full exposition of the concern, see the introduction and the preamble to Resolution 3-09, *ibid.,* pp. 133-138.

[6] Resolution 3-01, *ibid.,* pp. 127-128.

[7] Resolution 3-09, *ibid.,* pp. 133-139.

[8] Resolutions 3-12 and 3-12A, *ibid.,* pp. 140-142.

[9] Resolution 2-12, *ibid.,* pp. 114-115.

[10] *Ibid.,* p. 115.

[11] Resolution 5-03, *ibid.,* pp. 163-165, was intended to clarify Article VIII,C of Synod's Constitution: "All matters of doctrine and of conscience shall be decided only by the Word of God. All other matters shall be decided by a majority vote." Though it was discussed in two sessions, no action was taken.

[12] The Synod's Commission on Constitutional Matters grounded its ruling on By-law 4.01, having to do with rules of eligibility of pastors and teachers for a call, and on the prerequisites for ordination spelled out in By-law 4.15. Congregations and districts which called and ordained Seminex graduates appealed to the Synod's Constitution, Article VII. See the Synod's *Handbook, 1973,* pp. 17-18 and 97-99.

[13] 1 Kings 18:17-18; 19:14.

[14] 1 Kings 22:1-28.

[15] Jeremiah 4:10; 25:8-9; 38:4.

[16] Luke 3:19-20.

[17] Matthew 26:59-68.

[18] Acts 5:28.

[19] Acts 22:3-5.

[20] Article VIII,C. See note 11, above.

[21] Article II.

[22] John 16:8-15.

[23] Luke 24:25-27, 44-47.

[24] Augsburg Confession (AC) VII.

[25] In the paraphrasing which follows, we draw primarily on the translation of Luther's Small Catechism in Theodore G. Tappert, *The Book of Concord* (Philadelphia: Fortress Press, 1959), pp. 342-352.

[26] Large Catechism II, 42-43, *ibid.,* p. 416.

[27] AC V; Smalcald Articles (SA) III, viii, 3, 10; Formula of Concord, Solid Declaration (FC, SD) II, 4.

[28] "A Statement of Scriptural and Confessional Principles" (SSCP) IV,A. Though adopted by the Synod (note 6, above), SSCP was not printed in the *Proceedings* of the 1973 Convention or in the pre-Convention Workbook.

[29] "Someone recently suggested a term which may focus, better than any other, on the nub of the problem. He saw Missouri's difficulties as a struggle between Bible believers and Bible doubters. It's the kind of telling phrasing

which may well get wide usage." *Affirm*, III, No. 9 (February 28, 1974), 3.

[30] For example, in SA II,ii,15 Luther says, "The Word of God shall establish articles of faith and no one else, not even an angel." The reference to "not even an angel" makes it clear that Luther is thinking of the Word of God as meaning the Gospel (Gal. 1:8). Yet the context in the Smalcald Articles shows clearly that Luther has in mind the Scriptures. The simplest explanation would seem to be that Luther is thinking of the Scriptures and their authority in terms of the Gospel meaning of "the Word of God" (contrary to the understanding of this quotation in SSCP IV,C), yet nowhere do the Confessions detect or work through this kind of ambiguity.

[31] Apology (Ap) IV,2, German.

[32] SSCP, IV,C,4.

[33] SSCP, Conclusion.

[34] SSCP, IV,E,4.

[35] SSCP, IV,I,4. The principle is clearly illustrated by the second Resolved in Resolution 3-09 of the New Orleans Convention: "That the Synod repudiate that attitude toward Holy Scripture, particularly as regards its authority and clarity, which reduces to theological opinion or exegetical questions matters which are in fact clearly taught in Scripture." *Proceedings*, p. 139.

[36] *Ibid.*, p. 114.

[37] SSCP, Conclusion.

[38] Thus in its section on "Gospel Reductionism," the Preamble of Resolution 3-09 declares that "where the 'Gospel' is established as the 'governing principle' instead of the Scriptural Word, then such 'Gospelism' reduces to a minimum the content of Christian belief and discards whatever does not seem to serve it directly. . . . This often leads to an erosion of the Scripture's authority, especially as regards matters like 'history, geography, and nature . . .' " *Proceedings*, p. 136.

[39] Hymn 283, *The Lutheran Hymnal* (St. Louis: Concordia Publishing House, 1941).

[40] FC,SD,V,3-6.

[41] Num. 23:19; Prov. 30:5; John 8:32; 10:35; 15:26; 16:13; 17:17; Col. 1:5; Tit. 1:2; Heb. 6:18.

[42] Ps. 119:105; John 3:19-21; 8:46-47; 9:39-41; 2 Cor. 4:3-6; 2 Pet. 1:19.

[43] Ps. 33:6; Rom. 1:16; 1 Thess. 1:4; Heb. 4:12.

[44] John 14:6; 17:3: Acts 4:12; Gal. 1:8; Eph. 4:1-6; Deut. 5:6-11; 6:4-5.

[45] Luke 21:33; 1 Pet. 1:23-25.

[46] John 6:63; 1 Cor. 2:11-13; 2 Tim. 3:16; Heb. 4:12; 1 Pet. 1:23.

[47] SSCP,IV,D illustrates the confusion. "Because the Scriptures have God as their author, they possess . . . the divine power to make men wise unto salvation through faith in Jesus Christ." Notice that it is not the Gospel, the proclamation of forgiveness through Christ, which gives Scripture its power, but rather its divine authorship! By virtue of God's authorship again, and not the Gospel, the Scriptures have also "the divine authority to serve as the church's sole standard of doctrine and life (normative authority)." "Holy Scripture is powerful and efficacious," SSCP declares, but again, with no reference to the Gospel, even though the Scriptures themselves ascribe power solely to the Gospel (note 43, above). The separation between two authorities, and the secondary status of the Gospel's authority, is evident when SSCP then rejects the views: "1. That the authority of Scripture is limited to its

efficacy in bringing men to salvation in Jesus Christ. 2. That the authority of Scripture has reference only to what the Scriptures *do* (as means of grace) rather than to what they *are* (as the inspired Word of God)."

[48] Matt. 7:24-25; 24:35.

[49] "A view of the Scriptures which puts the Scriptures at the mercy of man's reason, and teaches that the Scripture errs must ultimately put also the message of the Gospel at the mercy of the same human reason and render that message unsure" (1973 *Proceedings*, p. 62). The logical sequence puts Scripture first, the Gospel second. The Gospel message as the Spirit's testimony to Christ is not sure in itself. Its sureness is secondary, dependent upon and derived from the prior sureness of the inerrant Bible.

[50] "These [questions] involved such matters as . . . the origin, nature, and authority of Scripture. The Convention must decide what it wants. Someone ought to have the authority to determine who should supervise doctrine and how our faith should be interpreted. We must retain the authority of the synodical voice and allow our officials to act. We should not delude ourselves to what is at stake." *Ibid.,* p. 26.

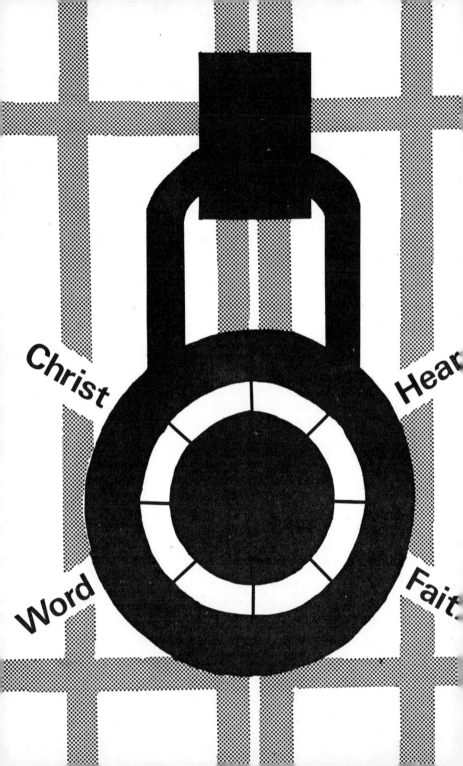

Chapter II

The Word of Spirit and Life

Every man's work, though built on the foundation of Jesus Christ, must be tested by fire, Paul says.[1] Therefore every diagnosis of Synod's dross, including our own, is bound to experience such testing through brethren who resist, challenge, and wrestle with it. That is all to the good. God promises that His purifying fire shall not cease among us until He has "accomplished the intents of his mind" (Jer. 30:24) and thus overthrown any "intents" which are merely man's.

Meanwhile, with confidence in the Lord's ruling hand and with such gifts as He gives us, we may begin to look beyond the fire. Let us envision a day when the dross has been exposed and separated out of us, and when the Spirit of Christ has thereby cleansed and renewed the church which is His body. On that day what will Lutheran education have become?

For a simple definition of what Lutheran education ought to be and do, we may well turn to Luther's explanation of the first petition (Small Catechism).

> God's name is hallowed [the climate and character of Lutheran education] when the Word of God is taught clearly and purely [the method] and we, as children of God, lead holy lives in accordance with it [the goal].[2]

In its concern for education our Synod has always dedicated itself to teaching the Word of God clearly and purely. Now, however, the Lord's fire is exposing a subtle dross which has marred our very conception of "the Word of God." As a result we have in reality not been teaching the Word of God as clearly and purely as we thought or wanted. We did it "in ignorance," as Peter would say. Once the dross is revealed, however, we must be ready to let it go in "repentance," "that your sins may be blotted out, that times of refreshing may come from the presence of the Lord" (Acts 3:17, 19).

What will it mean to teach "clearly and purely" that Word of God which Luther knew, and which is the very genius of Lutheran education? Our resource to search that question is Scripture, "the pure and clear fountain of Israel" and our "only true norm." [3] We have the advantage also of the Lutheran Confessions, whose insight into the Gospel will continually control and test our understanding of Scripture.

We shall explore the Gospel meaning of the Word of God by pointing to four distinct and indispensable themes. They are like four precise stopping points on a combination lock. When the dial has turned properly to each designated point, the Gospel is pure, the lock opens, and the prisoner is set free. If any stopping point on the lock is omitted or blurred, or if false stopping points are substituted or interposed, then the Gospel is not being "taught clearly and purely." Then hearts imprisoned in flesh and sin, law and death, are not fully free. To know the right combination, not only in mind but above all in the heart through the Spirit, is to have the pure Gospel. To know this combination is also to know the Scriptures, for that is what the Bible as the Word of God is all about. To know it is to share also in the true glory of the Lutheran Confessions.

CHRIST'S HONOR AS THE ONLY SAVIOR (CHRIST ALONE)

The first two positions on our dial are frequently mentioned together in the Confessions as a kind of matching pair. Between them they provide a critical test for what is truly the Gospel. Thus "justification" is called the "main doctrine of Christianity" which

> *illumines and magnifies the honor of Christ* and *brings pious consciences the abundant consolation* that they need. Our opponents [the confessors continue] confuse this doctrine miserably, they *obscure the glory and the blessings of Christ,* and they *rob pious consciences of the consolations offered them in Christ.*[4]

Let us therefore turn our dial first to the glory of Christ as the only Savior. It is a familiar theme also in the Scriptures. "No one comes to the Father, but by me," Jesus says (John 14:6). Peter testifies boldly that

> there is salvation in no one else, for there is no other name under heaven given among men by which we must be saved (Acts 4:12).

26

Paul wants to glory in nothing "except in the cross of our Lord Jesus Christ" (Gal. 6:14). "For if justification were through the law," he says, "then Christ died to no purpose" (Gal. 2:21). Such texts are more than doctrinal assertions, however. They assume and testify to a history—above all, the climactic history of Jesus' death. "We preach Christ crucified," Paul declares, for in that visible person and event we come to know "the power of God and the wisdom of God" (1 Cor. 1:23-24). Jesus' death (with His resurrection) is the historical turning point at which the Old Testament abruptly ends and the New Testament begins.[5] Therefore the passion history is our key access to "the gospel of the glory of Christ who is the likeness of God" (2 Cor. 4:4).

We need to see in Jesus' death what the apostles saw, namely, how our salvation unfolds in the very way that event happened. Jesus came to Jerusalem to confront the nation in its leaders with a last call to repent before the day of the kingdom brought utter destruction, but the city did not repent.[6] Zealotic crowds, with high expectation of the kingdom and its glory, hailed Jesus as the greater David. They waited eagerly for the flash of revelation and angelic intervention which would inaugurate the final overthrow of Israel's enemies. Caiaphas as High Priest was responsible for peace and order in Jerusalem at Passover time. Seeing the threat of fanatical insurrection surging around Jesus and anticipating the inevitable Roman retaliation, he proposed his cold and scarcely arguable strategy,

> It is expedient for you that one man should die for the people, and that the whole nation should not perish.[7]

Through Judas' intrigue the scene was set on the Mount of Olives [8] for the confrontation between the little band of hopeful disciples with their two swords and a battalion of armed officers, but the glory of God and the twelve legions of angels did not appear.[9] Jesus rejected the sword and surrendered himself for the disciples. "Let these men go," He said, wanting to lose not one.[10] The disciples escaped.

Thus Judas and his co-conspirators delivered Jesus up to Caiaphas, Caiaphas to Pilate, and Pilate to those who performed the crucifixion. Caiaphas' strategy was fulfilled. *One man died for the people*. The disciples, the temple and nation, even many Romans would have perished in the crushing consequence of a tragically misconceived zealotic revolt (as actually happened forty years later). In this moment of crisis, however, all were saved by the death of the innocent Jesus. Yet Jesus did not go to the cross as a martyred victim. He delivered Himself to death in love for his Father, for his disciples, for Jerusalem, and for His People, even for the Gentile invaders and enemies of Israel. "Father, forgive them" He prayed (Luke 23:34). Caiaphas' strategy was not really his own after all! By it God was accomplishing His purpose.[11] God the Father gave his Son a bitter cup to drink,[12] but with it also a promise. Jesus would not lose His life but find it, and not only His life but also the lives of those He loved.[13] The Father would raise Him up on the third day.[14] In defiance of death and of the wisdom and verdict of the sinners, the Father would give Him the Kingdom.[15]

We can see all of this and much more in the *visible* history. Beyond what men could witness, however, lay another dimension of reality, made visible to us through God's Word and Spirit. The climactic day of the cross was more than a human event. It was the day of the Lord, of judgment and of salvation, when the Kingdom arrived whose imminent coming John the Baptist and Jesus had proclaimed.[16] The Ancient of Days sat in judgment, and the books were opened.[17] All mankind was now divided before the Lord, wheat from chaff, sheep from goats.[18] At the Lord's left stood the totality of ungodly humanity, not the Gentiles only but also the Jews, including even Jesus' own disciples. None was righteous, not one.[19] Only one man stood at God's right hand, the beloved Son who loved and trusted and served the Father with all His heart. Shall the Lord go through with His judgment and justice, turn loose the fury of His wrath to destroy the whole world, and give the Kingdom to the one righteous Son who alone can inherit it? The Father's steadfast love will not allow it.

> I am God and not man, the Holy One in your midst, and I will not come to destroy (Hos. 11:9).

Thus the God of all grace speaks to His Son. Jesus consents to drink the cup of wrath which had been prepared for Jerusalem and all nations.[20] Therefore the salvation purchased by Jesus' blood in the visible political realm is in reality cosmic. What threatened the world in the week we call "holy" was not merely zealotic war and bloody Roman retaliation, but the universal wrath of God. Jesus swallowed God's wrath in his own dying! His one death is therefore both sacrifice and atonement, the end of the world and its beginning. It is the source of life and redemption not only for Israel but for the world, and not only for one generation but for humanity in all generations. This is the glory, full of grace and truth, which we are given to behold now and forever.[21] God was in Christ, reconciling the world to Himself, making Him who knew no sin to be sin for us.[22] In this the love of God was made manifest among us.[23]

Jesus' resurrection speaks God's verdict, exposes the truth, opens the Scriptures, and pours out the Spirit. He comes to His disciples to lift them out of death into life, and to send them out as ambassadors of reconciliation for the whole world. Their proclamation does not create the history. On the contrary, the history through the Spirit generates their proclamation.[24]

This history itself, and the Spirit in the history, demands that Christ have His full honor as Savior. There is no history like it. Jesus is not a myth or a symbolical representation. We evade and lose His real glory if we attach His essential honor to His teaching, or to His works of love, or to His miracles, or even to His incarnation *apart from the cross*. In the cross, in what appears to be His total defeat and shame, is revealed the glory and victory of Jesus' and the Father's love! That is why the Sacrament of the Altar keeps bringing us back to the body and blood of His death. Jesus is not one name among many, or one martyr among many, or one truth among many, or one love among many. All such generalization evades the uniqueness of His history and robs Him of His honor. But when the only Son is not given His honor, then the Father is not known or honored either.[25] For the Father invites us to see and know Him in the cross of His Son, and nowhere else. There is no getting around the cross!

Here is the truth in Christ which makes us free! Lutheran education after the purifying will not be ashamed of or equivocate about the cross. It will delight to proclaim the glory of God in Jesus Christ crucified.

THE SINNER AND HIS TERRORS OF CONSCIENCE
(GRACE ALONE)

The dial of our combination lock turns back, twice around to the left as it were, and stops at the anxious conscience. We are looking now at the target of the Word of God, the inmost personhood of the sinner, his heart or conscience. For it is to terrified hearts that the Gospel of Christ addresses its comfort. The terrified heart is a very significant theme in the Lutheran Confessions. For example,

> It is a matter of experience that weak and terrified consciences find [this teaching of the Gospel] most comforting and salutary. The conscience cannot come to rest and peace through works, but only through faith . . . when it is assured and knows that for Christ's sake it has a gracious God. . . . [The Latin text adds] This whole teaching is to be referred to that conflict of the terrified conscience, nor can it be understood apart from that conflict.[26]

Lutheran education needs to understand this target, the heart or conscience of the sinner. Conscience involves more than merely guilt feelings. To speak of man's conscience is to reckon with his whole natural sinnerhood and hostility toward God. The heart is "full of evil lust," as the Confessions say, and "unable to have true fear of God and true faith in God." [27] Lutheran education will therefore seek to grasp more clearly the sharp distinction which Scripture and the Confessions draw between *sinners* who do not know God and the *righteous* who know and rest in Him. It is the same distinction which divides idolatry from true worship, and man in the flesh from man in the Spirit. The distinction has nothing to do with man's outward appearance or social status. It cuts through his inmost heart.

According to the diagnosis of many Biblical texts, we have no natural inclination or capacity whatsoever to know, trust, and serve God.[28] A new and clean heart comes only by God's gracious intervention, creation, and call. Thus God creates Israel as His people by calling them out of Egypt and naming them His first-born son.[29] Their status as His son (and not merely the forgiveness of what we think of as sin) constitutes Israel's "righteousness," just as our call and election to belong to God and His people in Christ is our righteousness. By that call the righteous know the God to whom

30

they now belong. They enter a new life. They are no longer slaves but sons. As sons they are to fear, love, and trust God with all their hearts.

Nevertheless the righteous, although created and called to be God's people, keep falling into sinnerhood. The story of the fall in Genesis 3 shows clearly what the force of sin is and how it works also in us. Instead of knowing God by hearing and believing what God has said to him, the sinner "knows good and evil." His eyes have been opened and he thinks he is wise. When he sees something desirable he calls it "good." He loves it and wants it, even if God has said he is not to have it. On the other hand, when he sees something distasteful or threatening, the sinner avoids it as "evil," even though God may be asking him to take the risk, endure the suffering, or bear the burden. Thus the sinner is "like God." He directs his life in God's world by his own eyesight and judgment, pursuing whatever looks good to him and fleeing what looks evil. Rather than fear, love, and trust God above anything else he fears the "evil," loves the "good," and trusts only himself.

It is not hard to see then why the sinner becomes anxious and why his heart experiences terrors. He has taken upon himself an enormous responsibility. He must constantly weigh advantage against disadvantage for himself. He discovers that he does not know with any guaranteed accuracy what is really "good" for him. The good he pursues eludes him or fails to yield the anticipated satisfaction. Often it traps him in an unexpected backlash of "evil." He escapes from one evil, a lion for example, only to find himself face to face with a bear.[30] The sinner is proud of his successes, but he never ceases to be insecure, anxious, and troubled.[31] Even if he turns to "god," the only god he knows is one he must placate or somehow harness to his own help and advantage. The sinner remains in control even of his god. He now bears the additional burden of saving his god and justifying his religion.[32] But if the sinner in his calculating wisdom decides that his religion is futile and not worth maintaining, he is right back where he started. He is forced to be his own god, his own creator, his own savior.

The sinner assumes responsibility for himself. He cannot know or accept his life as freely given by God, nor can he in humility and thanksgiving let God possess it, care for it, and rule it. He must defend his selfhood and dress himself up. If he suffers reverses he must find people or demons in the world to blame for his troubles.

Even if he achieves a measure of security and riches for the moment, however, the sinner does not escape anxiety. He is self-conscious. He worries about his worth. He assumes he is important, but has to prove his worth to himself and to the world. He must defend his dignity against any evidence that he is really worthless. Therefore he contrives to wrap himself in symbols of importance. He develops poise and learns how to maintain it in the face of adversity. He puts on tenuous "fig leaves" in the hope of making a good impression and of propping up his precarious worth. But he cannot escape his hidden anxiety, the fearful awareness that he is putting on a show, that he is really empty, and that the illusion may one day be found out.

Now the sinner confronts the problem we usually associate with "conscience." He is aware of being judged "under the law" as Paul puts it (Rom. 3:19). People are looking at him. They enforce expectations upon him and render verdicts. The sinner knows the verdict is coming and maneuvers for approval. A favorable verdict is a great "good," to be pursued with all diligence. A negative verdict is an "evil" to be avoided at all costs. Conscience turns the sinner alternately into a show-off and a liar. Behind conscience, whether he knows it or not, stands God doing his "alien work" of wrath.[33]

Man in sin is always under the Law. No alternative possibility is known to him. Being under the law, he can only maneuver for the favorable verdict, fall back on specious justifications and counter-accusations, or (if all else fails) yield to despair.

As Lutheran education comes to understand more fully the strivings and despair of the anxious conscience, it will be able to focus its Gospel more effectively to meet such terrors. Here Lutheran education possesses an advantage over psychology as a secular science. The researcher in psychology is limited by his own sinnerhood. He cannot question or criticize the natural wisdom which is so basic to all human experience, namely, the wisdom of "knowing good and evil." His own impulse, like that of every sinner, is to want whatever seems attractive and to avoid whatever seems repulsive, without any knowledge of the Word and wisdom of God. He does not recognize that this impulse, when it sets itself above the Word of God, is sin, and that it forces him to act in everything by his own judgment as though he himself were God. He cannot discover how he is now imprisoned under a pervasive regime of law and judgment which alternately builds up his pride or drives him into depression and despair. He is deceived and left empty by sin, death, and the law, but he does not know it. What God knows of human psychology as He "searches the hearts of men" [34] becomes knowable to us only when we have been delivered from sin and death and set free as sons and heirs of God in Christ through the Spirit.

Lutheran education's pure and clear Gospel will aim for the heart. There are "gospels" which address men at the point of their physical and social needs, their thinking minds, their moral conscience under the law, their emotional stresses, or their capacity for mystery and awe of the supernatural. These, however, are not yet God's Gospel! God's Gospel knows and is concerned for all these levels of our humanness, but it works from the inside out. *The point at which true freedom and transformation occur through the Spirit, where the consolation happens which makes all things new, is the anxious heart or terrified conscience.* The Confessions know this. The Scriptures know it. Lutheran education needs to know it with increasing clarity, insight, and joy as the ultimate target of all its work. If anyone does not understand this in his own experience and heart, however, both Scripture and the Confessions lose their focus for his as "the Word of God" and become simply a pious blur.

THE WORD OF GOD (SCRIPTURE ALONE)

We turned our dial first to the honor of Christ, then to the anxious conscience of the sinner. Now we dial right again, and stop at the Word of divine grace and promise. It is by words that the Holy Spirit brings God's glory in Christ to bear on the troubled heart of the sinner so as to set him free. In our Synod's crisis nothing is more important for Lutheran education than to understand anew what Scripture and the Confessions mean when they speak of "the Word of God."

In the Confessions, the Word and the sacraments are the means by which sinners come to know and rest in a gracious God. Immediately after speaking of Christ and Justification, the Augsburg

33

Confusion continues with an article on the Word:

> To obtain such faith God instituted the office of the ministry, that is, provided *the Gospel and the sacraments.* Through these, as through means, He gives the Holy Spirit, who works faith, when and where he pleases, in those who hear the Gospel.[35]

The presence and use of the Word of God identifies the church, for its "outward marks" are "the Word and the sacraments."[36] By definition the church is

> the assembly of believers among whom the Gospel is preached in its purity and the holy sacraments are administered according to the Gospel.[37]

Therefore the power of bishops in the church is simply

> a power and command of God to preach the Gospel, to forgive and retain sins, and to administer and distribute the sacraments.[38]

Although God uses men to speak His Gospel, the Word they speak is and remains God's.

> The Word of absolution . . . is not the voice or word of the man who speaks it, but it is *the Word of God,* who forgives sin, for it is spoken in God's stead and by God's command. . . . God requires us to believe this absolution as much as if we heard *God's voice from heaven,* that we should joyfully comfort ourselves with absolution.[39]

The imagery of the voice from heaven derives, of course, from the Scriptures. "I have talked with you from heaven," says the Lord at Sinai (Ex. 20:22). An angel flies "in mid-heaven, with an *everlasting Gospel to proclaim* to those who dwell on earth" (Rev. 14:6). The voice of that Gospel is always from heaven, even if its instrument is men. Paul says as much,

> Our Gospel came to you not only in Word, but also in power and in the Holy Spirit and with full conviction (1 Thess. 1:5).

Later he adds,

> When you received the Word of God which you heard from us, you accepted it not as the word of men but as what it really is, the Word of God, which is at work in you believers (1 Thess. 2:13).

The Thessalonians had ears in their hearts. By those ears they heard the voice of God.

We entrust that miracle of hearing to the Spirit. Our concern here, and the concern of a purified Lutheran education, has to be for the substance of the message. It will not do to call something "the Word

34

of God" which does not, in fact, belong to His Word. We must therefore know clearly *what God is really saying* and what He has given us authority to proclaim and teach in His name. He calls us to teach His Word fully, uncompromisingly, subtracting nothing from it. At the same time He warns us not to add to His Word, not to invoke the name of the living God on words which are merely the product of man's wisdom and reasoning. "What has straw in common with wheat? says the Lord" (Jer. 23:28).

We do not know the living Word of God simply by reading the Bible or by studying Christian doctrine. We know it by the miracle of the Spirit, when the wisdom and mercy of God through that Word has broken into our hearts to make everything alive and new. When that happens to us we know more than merely words, ideas, and doctrines. We know God and rest joyfully in His grace. We are not of the flesh any more, but of the Spirit, not slaves but free. God has named us His *"sons."* In "the spirit of sonship" we cry "Abba! Father!" "The Spirit bears witness with our spirit that we are children of God." If we are sons, however, we are immediately also God's "heirs." As His children and heirs we are also invited to *serve* and suffer with Christ while waiting to be glorified with Him (Rom. 8:14-17). The whole substance of the Word of God in Scriptures and Confessions is gathered here under the threefold and closely intertwined themes of our sonship, inheritance, and servanthood. Let us unfold these further, one by one.

The Word That Names Us God's Sons [40]

"You are my beloved son," the voice from heaven declared to Jesus (Mark 1:11). That word now speaks also to us, for we have been baptized into His name. Sonship is, of course, only one of many imageries which the Scriptures employ to establish and affirm our relationship to God and to His people. We are also named God's vineyard,[41] His elect or chosen people,[42] His special possession.[43] We are the "righteous" who know and belong to God,[44] in contrast to the "sinners" we were before.[45]

English translations tend to lose the linguistic link (so obvious in Greek) between "righteousness" and "justification." To be "justified" is to be made "righteous," that is, to be taken fully into God's family.[46] It is to receive the sonship [47] as the lost son was gathered home by the father's love and called *worthy, alive, found,* and *my son.*[48] Hence "forgiveness of sins" implies more than remission of guilt and punishment. Forgiveness establishes and confirms the relationship of sons to the Father, and thus also of brother to brother. Barriers are down. Accusations cease. Love shines. By the baptism which "forgives sins" (Mark 1:4) and clothes us in Christ, we "are all sons of God through faith" (Gal. 3:26-27). Since all of us are gathered equally into God's family, we are also brothers of one another. No one is superior or inferior to any other. "If you are Christ's, then you are Abraham's offspring, heirs according to promise" (Gal. 3:29).

Lutheran education will "mine" the Scriptures eagerly for the variety of imageries which we subsume here under the Word of "sonship." Yet all such searching serves only one goal, namely, that out of these treasures the Word of God may be taught clearly and purely, for the hallowing of God's name and for the comfort of terrified and empty hearts. The heart of the sinner "thirsts for God, for the living God" (Ps. 42:2). Jesus picks up the metaphor when He calls His Word the "living water" and promises that those who drink it will "never thirst." Indeed, once a man has drunk this water of life, it becomes in him a well which pours out the same comfort and Spirit to others who thirst for it.[49] For the Word of God refreshes the thirsty heart and gives it rest from all its terrors.

Does the terrified heart feel ashamed and guilty, oppressed and bound under law? Does the sinner look upon himself as worthless, inadequate, futile, and inferior? Is he despised, lonely, and desperate for praise? Does he fight his basic insecurities by attacking others, or hide them under a show of poise and self-confidence, as though he had everything under control? The Word of God brings the sinner down from every mountain of pride, and lifts him up from every valley of despair. "I am your worth, your portion, your eternal treasure," God declares. "I have delivered you from all judgment and brought you to myself, for my love's sake and through the cross of Christ. You are my beloved son. That is the name by which I have called you to be mine. And no one shall pluck you out of my hand!" [50]

The Word of God makes the worthless worthy, and the unimportant eternally important. It utterly refutes the standards by which men measure themselves and one another. It turns the natural wisdom of man into foolishness. Paul captures the drama of the great reversal:

> God chose what is low and despised in the world, even things that are not, to bring to nothing things that are. . . . Therefore, as it is written, "Let him who boasts, boast of the Lord" (1 Cor. 1:28-30).[51]

As for the sinner's guilt and fear of accusation under the law, God does far more than merely erase sins. In Christ's death the whole system of law under which we were bound is abolished. Judgment Day is past and gone! The threatened "Day of the Lord" so full of wrath and terrors was fulfilled on Good Friday.[52] By His death Jesus stood in the breach and swallowed up every indictment that should have destroyed us. For us "the Lord's Day" is now Easter, with all the grace and peace revealed to us in His Resurrection.[53] "No condemnation for those who are in Christ Jesus," is the final verdict (Rom. 8:1). "You are not under law, but under grace" (Rom. 6:14). "Who shall bring any charge against God's elect? It is God who justifies" (Rom. 8:33). The legal system which compelled us to strive for compliments and to flee from accusations is cancelled, nailed to the cross.[54] Not sin and law, but *grace reigns* "through righteousness to eternal life through Jesus Christ our Lord" (Rom. 5:21). *It is a whole new world of life and freedom that God offers and creates by His Word!*

Also the terrors of the sinner in the face of meaninglessness, futility, and emptiness are relieved by "the Word of God." For we know God! He is our Origin and our Destiny, our Alpha and Omega, from whom we came and to whom we return, in whom we "live and move and have our being" as his "offspring." [55] As Jesus came into the world from the Father, and again left the world to go to the Father, so do we in Him. By God's Word and Spirit everything that was Christ's is made ours.[56] Therefore we do not seek our "weight of glory" in

> the things that are seen but in the things that are unseen; for the things that are seen are transient, but the things that are unseen are eternal (2 Cor. 4:18).

Even when the limitless waters of the flood had negated all creation, Noah still had a harbor from which he came and to which he would

37

return, namely, his God. The Word of God creates harbors where the eye sees none!

The Word That Promises Us Our Inheritance

The Word of sonship already implies that we have an inheritance coming. "If children, then heirs," says Paul (Rom. 8:17). The Word that makes us children of God comes to us out of the *past,* as it were, from the history of Calvary sealed in our Baptism. The Word of inheritance comes from the *future.* It points ahead to a fulfillment which will turn even defeat into victory through the Resurrection of Christ.

The wide variety of "eschatological" (last things) texts in Scripture belong to this second aspect of God's Word. We cannot explore them here, nor can we attempt to integrate so many images of promise into a composite that is comprehensible to our minds. It is enough to rejoice that "death is swallowed up in victory," its sting and power broken, and to celebrate the God "who gives us the victory through our Lord Jesus Christ" (1 Cor. 15:54-56). We already share His Resurrection. He has prepared rooms for us in His Father's home.[57]

The Word of ultimate triumph conveys the assurance of God's care also for every unfolding tomorrow. "Fear not," God says. His promises hold us secure in the face of every dread, disaster, or helplessness. "No evil shall touch you" (Job 5:19), says the God who "knows good and evil" for us by a mercy that far transcends our calculating sight. Thus we trust God as our Father. He gives good gifts to His children, hears their cry, leads them through the valley of the shadow, and surrounds them with His goodness and mercy all the days of their life.

By such promises we rest in God, look to Him for all good, and turn to Him for refuge in every distress. We can pray with confidence not only "Give us each day our daily bread" (and thus give Him thanks for the continual outpouring of His good gifts), but also "Deliver us from evil." When we bear burdens beyond our comprehension, it often does not seem possible that God knows what He is doing with His peculiar "knowledge of good and evil." The evidences cry that God is not good after all, or that His wrath is kindled against us, or that He has utterly forsaken us. But the promises stand sure. They invite us to flee to God's breast like a trusting child and to pray by faith against sight, "O give thanks to the Lord, for *He is good!*" (Ps. 118:1).

The Word That Calls Us to Serve God Only

God has named us his sons. He has promised to be our God every day of our lives until He gives us our inheritance. Now we hear the third aspect of the Word of God. God calls us to serve Him only. "Let *my son* go, that he may *serve me,*" the Lord said to Pharaoh (Ex. 4:23). To be God's son is to take the form of a servant. "Righteousness" as an identity term has immediate implications for all of life. It points to a newness of heart and attitude, to a lifestyle by which we imitate the personality of God the Father.

God's Word of wisdom and commandment unfolds what His way of righteousness is like, in contrast to the way of the sinner.

Be merciful, even as your Father is merciful (Luke 6:36).

Be kind to one another, tenderhearted, forgiving one another, as God in Christ forgave you. Therefore be imitators of God, as beloved children. And walk in love, as Christ loved us (Eph. 4:32-5:1).

You shall be holy [that is, separated, different]; for I the Lord your God am holy (Lev. 19:2).

Since the righteous are "not under the law but under grace" (Rom. 6:14), God's law and commandment no longer conveys threat and judgment. It is rather a treasure of divine wisdom "more to be desired than gold . . . sweeter than honey" which revives the soul, "making the wise the simple . . . rejoicing the heart . . . enlightening the eyes" (Ps. 19:10, 7-9). Even when it "warns" God's servant (Ps. 19:11), this law belongs to the welcomed "good news," and not to God's accusing wrath. A new world has opened, a world controlled not by what the sinner calculates "good and evil" to be, but by the heavenly Father who "knows the way of the righteous" (Ps. 1:5), and whose love never fails. Jesus knew that way, and walked in it. To us He says, "Follow Me!" Even if it means taking the cross and losing your life, follow Me! For the way of the Father is life to you." [58]

Frequently in Scripture the way of the Lord is pictured as a straight line, from which God's holy people are not to "turn aside to the right

39

hand or to the left" (Deut. 5:32). We may appreciate, then, the Biblical contrast between man whom God made to walk upright with his eyes on God, and the serpent who slithers so cleverly on his belly to the right hand and to the left. To fall into sinnerhood is to adopt the way of the serpent. When the sinner sees something attractive and "good," he slithers crookedly to the right to grab for it (lust). When he encounters some obstacle which threatens trouble or "evil" to him, he slithers evasively to the left (fear). The sinner imagines that he is achieving advantage, life, and peace by such maneuvering, but the reality is deadly. "They have made their roads crooked, no one who goes in them knows peace" (Is. 59:8).

Summation: The Word of God in Its Three Aspects

"You are my son, my heir, my servant." Out of the past, out of the future, and into each present moment comes the divine Word by which God names us His own, holds eternal promises before us, and sets us on the way of true life. These three aspects belong together. If the commandments that describe servanthood are separated from the Word of sonship and of promise, for example, they immediately become moralistic and accusing law. In that case we are imprisoned under the law once again, driven by the law to demonstrate our superiority over sinners worse than ourselves, caught in a guilt we must always evade so as to save ourselves from despair.

This threefold Word is what the Confessions know as the Gospel in distinction from the Law. For the sake of this Law-Gospel Word we treasure the Holy Scriptures as the Word of God.[59] The miracle of God's Spirit in Martin Luther and the Reformation was not the discovery of the Bible or of reverance for its inspiration. The church had had the Scriptures and had reverenced them all along. Luther, however, through his study of the Scriptures and by the gift of the Spirit in that Word, began to hear clearly again what the God of everlasting grace was really saying to terrified hearts. By that discovery the pure Gospel was separated out from the dross of tradition and piety which had obscured its glory. The Lord put Luther himself through the pain of His purifying fire, so that through Luther the fire could be kindled throughout the church of his day. That was God's way of accomplishing the purifying He intended.

Once they had come through the pain of their own purifying, the

Lutheran Confessors rejected the authority of tradition. They could not submit any longer to mere ecclesiastical pressure or political power. They took their stand on the Scriptures alone. They knew what it meant to walk God's straight way, trusting their fears to Him. No enticement or threats of Pope or empire could induce them to swerve to the right hand or to the left. In standing on the Scriptures alone, they were standing on the pure Gospel of Christ. Their hearts had been comforted by that Gospel. In it they had found life and the knowledge of a gracious God.

If we subscribe to the Confessions today, we stand where the Confessors stood and add our joyful AMEN to theirs. We know and confess the Gospel in its truth and purity, and the Scriptures in their true glory as "the Word of God." For "the Word of God," whether Gospel or Scripture, does not have two meanings. There is only one Word of God. It is that Word which gives Christ His honor as the only Savior, and thereby truly comforts terrified consciences. It is the Word by which God declares us to be His sons for Christ's sake, promises us an inheritance which no power of earth or hell can take from us, and opens to us the joy and freedom of serving Him only. That Word in all its interwoven aspects, breaking through from the cross to our hearts by the Spirit, and overcoming all the tyranny of the law, is what Paul calls "the whole counsel of God" (Acts 20:27). That Word encompasses all our existence. There *is* nothing more.

Through the purifying, Lutheran education will rediscover the fullness and purity of that Word, and will *want* nothing more.

FAITH: THE HEART'S "YES" TO GOD THROUGH HIS WORD (FAITH ALONE)

The dial of our combination lock has stopped successively at the honor of Christ, the anxious conscience, and the Word of God. Now it almost leaps, as it were, to its final stopping point so that the lock may spring open and the prisoner be free. That final stop is faith. By faith the conscience comes to "rest and peace . . . when it is assured and knows that for Christ's sake it has a gracious God." [60]

In the Confessions the terms "justification by grace through faith" or "the righteousness of faith" become summary titles for the whole Gospel.[61] The terminology derives particularly from Paul.[62] Although faith in association with righteousness is an Old Testament concept,[63] the term takes on a peculiar new force in the New Testament era. Paul contrasts "the righteousness of faith" sharply with "righteousness under the Law." [64] "Faith came" and "Christ came" are equivalents for him.[65] The foundations of justification (or righteousness) were revolutionized in the hour of judgment and salvation when Jesus died and rose again. The old marks of identity (blood lineage from Abraham, circumcision, the distinctive Jewish law) no longer signaled election and sonship. Jesus alone is the Son of God in truth. That is what His lonely passion and resurrection revealed. Thereafter the "power to become children of God" is given to all who "receive" Jesus, who *believe* in His name" who are "born, not of blood nor of the will of the flesh nor of the will of man, but of God" (John 1:12-13).

We can read between the lines how traumatic and painful the transition from Old to New Testament was for the Jews. Nicodemus protested against the necessity of being "born again." [66] Paul knew well what it meant to leave behind every old mark of fleshly descent and every advantage of Jewish law for the sake of righteousness in Christ alone.[67] For us, too, there is an old to be left behind, a "flesh" to which we even "die." It includes all the passions of desire and fear so natural to the sinner's knowledge of good and evil. Our passage from old to new is a great miracle of God's grace and Spirit. It happens when "faith" happens.

But "faith" happens through *words*. Faith comes by hearing "the Word of God" (Rom. 10:17 AV) or "the preaching of Christ" (RSV). The divine promise breaks through from the cross, calling the terrified heart to sonship, inheritance, and the glory of servanthood. The Word of life and hope is like a totally unexpected bread or water in the wilderness.[68] The starving or thirsty heart devours the message, finds life in it, and knows God by it. This is "faith." Faith is involuntary. It is not a product of conscious will or calculating decision. When the Father in Jesus' parable embraced, kissed, and clothed the lost son, that son suddenly found himself sitting at the banquet table and sharing the joy of the family. What made him go in, whereas his own brother, seemingly far more "worthy," would not go in? The answer does not lie in his own wisdom, or in eyes greedy for potential advantages. In the astonishing moment of mercy when the Father said "Come," to come was the obvious and only thing to do. That is "faith." Believing is not our doing. Faith simply happens in us, by the Spirit's call through the Gospel.

Lutheran education needs to make clear what "faith" is in relation to "the Word of God," and to Baptism and Holy Communion as sacraments of that Word. The goal of Lutheran education is faith. The method, therefore, requires a clear awareness that faith happens not in the thinking mind but in the terrified and thirsty heart. Faith is not the end product of instruction in a system of theology and doctrine. It is not a work or pattern of behavior. It does not come by anyone's will or desire to "have faith," neither can it be measured or detected by internal self-criticism. Faith is not a conviction of "truth" attained through a series of logical evidences and inferences. It is not instilled through respect for the authority of the teaching office. It is not "believing the Bible." It is not a quality of religious sensitivity or of capacity for intuition. Neither is faith generated, confirmed, or supported by extra-sensory perceptions or spiritual experiences apart from Christ and the Word of the cross. Faith is not a virtue which makes a person superior. Faith is not a minimal requirement to be met under some residual concept of Law.

A purified Lutheran education will know what faith really is. Faith is the simple yes and Amen of a heart liberated by the Word and Spirit of God. It is the miracle of eyes opened to see what God has prepared for those who love Him, which "no eye has seen, nor ear heard, nor the heart of man conceived" (1 Cor. 2:9-10). Faith has as its corollary "the Word of God," and cannot exist without that Word. Faith is the heart's eye looking away from self to the cross of Christ, and through the cross to the open arms and tender smile of the Father. When the Word that proclaims the grace of God in Christ is strong and clear, then the faith which knows God through that Word can be strong and clear. The Word of God is the Rock upon which we build our lives by faith. That Rock holds firm and unwavering through all the storms and testings of life, even against accusations that expose our sins and our doubts. For the promises of God do not fail. His love never grows weary. Heaven and earth will pass away, but His Word stands forever. By that Word we see God, trust Him, and rest in Him like a little child in the arms of its mother. By that Word we can walk God's way without being afraid. Therefore we love that Word and are eager to hear it. It is food and drink to us, the source of all joy and energy in the Spirit to bear God's kind of fruit in everything we do.

After the purifying, Lutheran education will know what a golden treasure the Word of God is, and will use it to comfort hearts and to set them free. By that understanding, itself a gift of the Spirit through the Word, Lutheran education will be equipped also to distinguish between "the spirit of truth and the spirit of error" (1 John 4:6), between what is truly God's Word and what is not.

This confronts us with some hard questions, however. We cannot avoid them. They belong to the purifying.

Footnotes for Chapter II

[1] 1 Cor. 3:10-15.
[2] Tappert, *op. cit.*, p. 346.
[3] FC,SD. Summary Formulation, 3.
[4] Ap IV,2-3.
[5] Matt. 26:28.
[6] Matt. 23:37.
[7] John 11:48-50.
[8] Zech. 14:3-9.
[9] Matt. 26:47-56; Luke 22:35-38, 47-53.
[10] John 18:8-9.
[11] John 11:51; Acts 2:23; 3:17; 4:28.
[12] Matt. 20:22; 26:39.
[13] Matt. 20:28.
[14] Hos. 6:2; Ps. 16:5-11.
[15] Matt. 22:44; 4:8-10; Luke 12:32.
[16] Matt. 3:2,10-12; 4:17.
[17] Dan. 7:9-14.
[18] Matt. 3:12; Ezek. 34:17; Matt. 25:32.
[19] Ps. 14:2-3.
[20] Jer. 25:15-29.
[21] John 1:14; 12:23-32.
[22] 2 Cor. 5:17-21.
[23] 1 John 4:9.
[24] John 15:26-27.
[25] John 5:23.
[26] AC XX, 15-17.
[27] AC II, on Original Sin. Also FC,SD I.
[28] Gen. 6:5; Ps. 51:5,10; Jer. 17:9; Matt. 15:19; Rom. 8:7-8.
[29] Is. 43:1; Hos. 11:1; Ex. 4:22-23.
[30] Amos 5:19.
[31] Matt. 6:33; Luke 10:41.
[32] Is. 46:1-2.
[33] Is. 28:21; Ap XII,51.
[34] Rom. 8:27; Rev. 2:23.
[35] AC V.

[36] Ap VII,7.

[37] AC VII,1.

[38] AC XXVIII,5.

[39] AC XXV,2-4.

[40] The Bible's language of "sonship" is extraordinarily useful for our purposes. Not only does it keep Jesus central as the turning point between Israel's sonship and ours (Gal. 3:23-4:7), but it also embraces within itself all three aspects of God's Word. The *son* is implicitly also heir and servant (Mark 12: 4-7).

In view of current concerns over sexism, however, it may be useful to point out that the Father-son language in Scripture, though grammatically "masculine," applies to the whole of God's people, male and female, as one holy family (Ex. 4:22; Hos. 11:1), without any consciousness of sexual distinctions. Indeed, the Scriptures seem perfectly free to ascribe to God the *Father* qualities and functions which belong in our thinking to *woman* and *mother!* God "bears" and "gives birth" to Israel (Deut. 32:18). He "conceives," "brings them forth," "carries them in His bosom as a nurse carries the sucking child" (Num. 11:12). He quiets our terrors, like a child quieted at its mother's breast (Ps. 131:2). God is the woman searching for a lost coin (Luke 15: 8-10). See also Is. 44:24; 45:10-11; 46:3; 49:14-15.

We shall use the sonship language freely, therefore, without any sexist connotation or self-consciousness. It would be altogether a distraction from the heart of Biblical concern, if we tried to find neutral terminology like "God–Person" for Father, and "child" for "son" (though the latter has ample Biblical warrant), or felt it necessary constantly to affirm womanhood by adding "or she" to every "he," and "or daughter" to every "son." The issue is sin and salvation, and here, in the Old Testament as well as in the New, there is "neither male nor female" (Gal. 3:28). "He fashioneth their hearts alike" (Ps. 33:15 AV). The very word "man" intends to embrace "male and female" (Gen. 1:27) in a unity which our individualistic and competitive culture, however, can neither comprehend nor enjoy. The problems of sexism derive from man's sin and alienation, not from Biblical language and thought.

[41] Is. 5:1-7; John 15:1-6.

[42] Deut. 7:5-9; 14:1-2; Eph. 1:4.

[43] Ex. 19:4-7; 1 Pet. 2:9-10.

[44] Gen. 15:6; Hab. 2:4; Gal. 3:6,11.

[45] Ps. 1:5; Matt. 9:13; Eph. 2:11-12.

[46] Luke 18:9-14.

[47] Gal. 4:5-7.

[48] Luke 15:22-24.

[49] John 4:14; 7:37-39.

[50] Ps. 16:5; 73:25-26; Is. 43:1; John 10:23-24.

[51] A paraphrase of Jer. 9:23–24.

[52] Amos 5:18; Joel 2:1-2; Zeph. 1:7-2:2.

[53] Rev. 1:10; John 20:19,26.

[54] Col. 2:14; Eph. 2:13-18.

[55] Rom. 11:36; Acts 17:28-29; Rev. 1:8.

[56] John 16:14-15, 27.

[57] John 11:25-26; 14:2.

[58] Luke 9:23-24.

[59] "All Scripture should be divided into these two chief doctrines, the law and the promises." Ap IV,5; FC,SD V. See also Ap XII,29-30.

[60] AC XX,15-16.

[61] AC IV; XXVII,38,48; XXVIII,62,64.

[62] Rom. 3:21-28; 4:13.

[63] Gen. 15:6; Hab. 2:4; Gal. 3:6,11.

[64] Rom. 9:30-10:8.

[65] Gal. 3:23-29.

[66] John 3:4.

[67] Phil. 3:2-11.

[68] Jer. 15:16; Is. 55:1-3; John 6:47-51.

Chapter III

Stumbling Blocks and Unbelief

The Lord's purifying fire will prove eminently worthwhile, if by it Lutheran education proclaims more clearly and richly that "most holy Gospel of the glory and grace of God" which Luther called "the true treasure of the church." [1]

In our previous chapter we amplified the meaning of that treasure from the perspective of faith and a transformed heart. We must now approach the Gospel from the opposite direction, namely, that of unbelief. As Lutheran education teaches Christ, a negative response to its witness is not necessarily a mark of failure. On the contrary, unbelief may even testify that the Word has been "taught clearly and purely." Unbelief is the authentic expression of the heart's natural hostility toward God.[2] Every true prophet and apostle, including Jesus Himself, has encountered it.[3]

Any effort to understand the dynamic of unbelief more clearly should serve to sharpen Lutheran education's proper "sword" and to keep it sharp (Heb. 4:12). However, there is an additional necessity for this inquiry. As the Lord's fire separates gold from dross among us, it is not enough that we rejoice in the purity of the gold. We must also know our dross, and how it has paraded as "the Word of God" among us, like a "fool's gold." A "dross-word" expects to be believed, after all. It begets a "dross-faith," over and above the Gospel's "one true faith." A dross-faith in turn begets a "dross-unbelief," for it diagnoses as "unbelief" every non-acceptance of the dross-word. Eventually such dross-faith may even elevate its dross-word as the standard of pure doctrine, and make it the criterion to determine who should or should not be trusted to teach the Word of God clearly and purely.

It will not do, therefore, to regard the teachings of the dross-word as a matter of indifference or of Christian freedom under the Gospel. The dross-word is the enemy of the Gospel. To permit it to stand unexposed and unchallenged is to tolerate error. We cannot consent to anything that compromises the pure doctrine of the Gospel or undermines the clarity and authority of the Scriptures as our only rule and norm.

If these thoughts have already begun to generate fear or anger, that very reaction testifies to the Lord's fire. But the fire must not be resisted or quenched. Comfort and safety are not to be found by hiding in the skirts of some higher authority. Teachers cannot evade the testing of what they teach by passing the responsibility to pastors. Pastors cannot evade it by claiming to be "only a simple pastor" and "not a theologian," and then referring the matter to the judgment of some specialized higher commission. Laymen and congregations cannot escape by relying on the majority wisdom and authority of a convention. No one shall excuse himself before God by preserving himself in ignorance or by blaming the dross on somebody else. "Every eye will see him" (Rev. 1:7). The time to see our Lord's hand is now, while His grace is so richly manifest even in the fire. To believe in Him and trust Him is to let Him have His way with us. For His promise stands sure:

> When you walk through fire and you shall not be burned, and the flame will not consume you (Isa. 43:2).

But if anyone will not trust God and deliver himself to the fire, he is setting his hope in the very dross the Lord is determined to destroy, and will perish with it.

When the purifying is finished, Lutheran education will be better able to see how deadly the dross has been. We are not safe from the kind of indictment Jesus spoke against Pharisaic education. The Pharisees won a convert, He said, only to make him "twice as much a child of hell" as themselves (Matt. 23:15). The Pharisees did not intentionally produce "children of hell" by their educational system any more than we would. Yet it happened. The dross did it. The greatest tragedy, however, was that when Jesus tried so openly to make them see their dross, they would not!

We call attention again to some serious questions Lutheran education faces. At the very least they are signals of a problem.

Why do Lutheran Christians, even when brought up in our schools, find it difficult to witness to the treasure in which they supposedly boast? Could it be in part that the dross mingled with the gold in their Gospel has obscured the riches of their own comfort? Or, since they believed the dross because they were told they *ought* to believe it, did they end up believing even the Gospl simply because they *ought* to?

50

Why do many young people drift so quickly into indifference? Are only family influences to blame? Why are some later "turned on for Christ" not through the church that nurtured them, but by encounter with people from other churches and movements?"

Why do many of our people come to abandon at least parts of what they are taught? We hear some say, "I know I was taught that, but I don't really believe it." And then, in order to salvage some authenticity of meaning in their faith, they turn to ideas derived from liberal thinkers and end up reconstructing their very understanding of Christianity. Perhaps whatever real "liberalism" exists in our church testifies not so much to "rationalism" (as the dross charges) as to a confusion and diminution of the Gospel caused by the dross itself.

Finally, how shall Lutheran education answer for the souls of people whose "faith" became to them not a ground of joy and freedom but a torment? "I went through real hell," we have heard some testify. "I felt I was an unbeliever facing eternal fire. I tried hard to believe what I had been taught, but I could not." And so, because a thoughtful child of God could not stop his God-given mind from thinking, he ended up rejecting not only the dross but the gold with it.

It is not our intention here to shroud Lutheran education in totally negative judgments. By God's grace we have indeed known and taught the Gospel with blessed effect through the Spirit, as many joyful saints will testify. Nevertheless, the fire that now rages within our Synod compels us to open our ears to the Word of the Lord, and to take seriously any evidence that something is amiss. Once we recognize that the fire is from the Lord, we need not fear it. We shall rather plead with Him to show us what we must see, so that He may remold us according to His blessed purpose.

Among His warnings to those involved in Lutheran education, is His word concerning the stumbling block. If anyone sets a stumbling block to trip up one of His little ones, says our Lord, "it would be better for him if a millstone were hung around his neck and he were cast into the sea" (Luke 17:1-2). The imagery of the stumbling block traces to Lev. 19:14, "You shall not put a stumbling block in the way of the blind," a tactic which a perverse and loveless sense of humor might consider "funny." Ordinarily in Scripture, however, a stumbling block stands for something that causes unbelief. It trips

a person up, so that he does not really hear what God's Word is saying, or follow in the way of God's life and kingdom.

A stumbling block in this latter sense may be authentic or inauthentic. On the one hand the very word of God's pure Gospel is
a stumbling block to the sinner who will not hear it.[4] Jesus Himself
is simultaneously the cornerstone for those who believe in Him and
a stone of stumbling for those who do not.[5] We shall need to explore
why this is so. On the other hand there are also inauthentic stumbling
blocks which the very teachers of God's Word set in the way of their
hearers. We shall have to examine also these.

Paul understood the true stumbling block of the Gospel as well as
the alien stumbling blocks which can so easily trip up God's saints
and divide them from one another. In Rom. 16:17 he refers to both:

> I appeal to you, brethren, to take note of those who create dissen-
> sions and difficulties [Greek: stumbling blocks] in opposition to the
> doctrine which you have been taught; and avoid them.

"The doctrine you have been taught" is the pure Gospel. That Gospel, as Paul implies here and states clearly elsewhere, is a stumbling
block in its own right.[6] As such it necessarily "creates dissensions"
between the Spirit and the flesh, and between the church and the
world. But if any other stumbling block is set within the church to
divide the very people whom Christ's Gospel has gathered and
united, that stumbling block together with those who create it must
be recognized and avoided.[7]

THE AUTHENTIC STUMBLING BLOCK:
THE GOSPEL

In the previous chapter we unfolded the message of the Word
of God in three aspects: sonship, inheritance, and servanthood. Each
of these proves to be a stumbling block to our natural heart. All
three are subsumed in what Paul calls the stumbling block of the
cross.[8]

The Word of Sonship as a Stumbling Block

By the Word of sonship God declares that we are no longer sinners
and outsiders under wrath, but members of His household. We are
forgiven, justified, elect, and gathered into our Father's family, not
by any right of our own, however, but purely by grace for Christ's

sake. God's Word confers on us a name of everlasting honor. No longer do we feel compelled to make a name for ourselves, or to win approval, or to be right, or to cover our wrongness. Our warfare is accomplished, our iniquity is pardoned.[9] We are saved, safe, and at rest. No enemy can accuse us or snatch us out of our Father's hand.[10]

To our natural independence and pride, however, that very Word proves to be a stumbling block. God calls us to surrender any illusion that we can impress Him as we impress people. To "repent" means to give up any such self-made importance. There is nothing in us by which we can attract God or win His admiration. We have no claim on Him, no resources with which to negotiate. God has stooped rather to pick us up out of an ash heap of nothingness and shame. He has had mercy on us even when we were the chief of sinners.[11] Therefore our natural self-esteem is shattered. We understand what the Magnificat means, "He has scattered the proud . . . put down the mighty . . . sent the rich away empty" (Luke 1:51-53).

The Pharisees illustrate what a stumbling block this Word really is. They justified themselves "before men," as Jesus acknowledges, and were held in high esteem. How then could Jesus possibly call their recognized and exemplary obedience "an abomination in the sight of God" (Luke 16:15)? The Pharisees were self-conscious about their rights, and concerned for signals of rank in seating arrangements.[12] They were sure that God would take due notice of their faithfulness to His Law.[13] They conceded that God could forgive sinners and take in whomever He pleased,[14] but not in such a way as to compromise their status. Therefore they could not comprehend the baptism by which John had gathered and justified sinners,[15] or the mercy by which Jesus even ate meals in their houses.[16] The Pharisees are the elder son in Jesus' parable, who sees only injustice in the Father's mercy to his brother. What good is faithful and dedicated service to God, if at the last minute any sinner can enter the kingdom and even have a joyful banquet to celebrate his homecoming? Surely God will be, if anything, *fair*![17]

It is natural for human hearts to measure everything in terms of justice and rights. We ourselves cannot trust or comprehend mercy any more than the Pharisees could. We can understand then how so natural a concern for fairness and rights could creep into the religious thinking of the Pharisees until it became even the determining factor. In the name of "Moses" a tradition developed which grounded much of piety in the distinction between clean and unclean, kosher and nonkosher. (Kosher is a later Yiddish term, but helps us recapture the depth of their feelings.) It was kosher to be a pure-blooded descendant of Abraham and to recite one's geneology all the way back to the Patriarch. It was kosher to be circumcized, to eat approved foods, to wash hands before meals, to rest on the Sabbath, to wear properly fringed garments, and to avoid contact with everything and anybody nonkosher. Kosherness constituted a claim on God. It testified to religious seriousness against all compromising idolatry.

John the Baptist and Jesus seemed to make light of the kosher and even to violate it. "God can make children of Abraham out of these stones," John said (Matt. 3:9). Jesus could touch a leper or the bier of a dead man without a qualm. He was not offended at the touch of a hemorrhaging woman. He was ready to enter the house of Gentiles as well as sinners within Israel. He was "loose" in observing the Sabbath. Since His ancestry, being Galilean, was mixed, the Pharisees felt justified in applying to Him the epithet "Samaritan." By their law it was easy to see Jesus as devil-possessed, a sinner and blasphemer who contradicted the justice of God's Law, a usurper of divine prerogatives, and a bold-faced liar who dared to identify Himself, His Word, and His work with God His Father.[18]

Jesus responded by exposing their stumbling block. By their "tradition," he said, they "made void the Word of God" (Matt. 15:6). Behind their observance of the kosher, they concealed hearts full of "evil thoughts, . . . false witness, slander" (Matt. 15:16). By invoking their tradition they were able to evade the most obvious commandments to love God with all their heart and to love their lost and sinful "neighbor" as themselves. The Pharisees could not have it both ways. Jesus pressed the case until they were forced to expose what master they really served.[19]

Lutheran education will view the Pharisees with great compassion. Their stumbling block simply exhibits our own. Our natural impulse too is to set our hope on rights, justice, and fairness. To preach the Gospel clearly and purely, therefore, we need to expose and magnify the stumbling block, so that the mercy of God may be truly mercy and not some bargaining compromise with our ideas of justice. The risk in that kind of teaching is that some hearers will trip over it. If so, however, their very unbelief will testify that the Gospel they heard was taught clearly and purely.

The Word of Inheritance as a Stumbling Block

As "sons" in God's household, we are also heirs of His eternal promises. We need not fear, for a kingdom is in store which the Father delights to give to His "little flock" (Luke 12:32). Kingdom, eternal life, and a room with Jesus in the Father's house, these are all images of the inheritance to come. The promises are assured to us, and no power in heaven or on earth will keep us from having them, not even death.[20]

The fulfillment of this promise, however, comes by God's mercy alone. It is not a reward of wages, as though we could earn or qualify for it through our strivings. God's kingdom has no continuity with the strivings or creativity of man. It stands apart as a new creation. It is full of glory and life, of vindication and victory. No one who trusts and waits for such promises of the Father will be caught short or left empty. God's Word pledges also that our Father will lead and walk with us in all the in-between days. He will give us every good gift and deliver us from every evil. Therefore we need not fear defeat or futility. We simply walk with our God, give Him thanks, harness our gifts in His service, submit all our own planning to His will and blessing, respond each day to opportunities as He unfolds them, turn to Him in trouble, and wait expectantly for each tomorrow as one more great gift from Him.

But, as Lutheran education must recognize, there lies also the stumbling block. Our natural hearts do not want to surrender to God or trust His promises that way. We want to be independent and responsible for ourselves. We find *dignity* in paying our own way, and regard it as cheap and unworthy to get everything for nothing. We find *security* in measuring what we have *now* against what is merely promised, and in deciding for ourselves what is the most advantageous choice. We trust what we can see with our own eyes, and hold suspect what we cannot see and control. After all, how do we *know* that the resurrection and a kingdom even exist?

In the drama of Jesus the stumbling block of the promised kingdom exhibited itself in various ways. From the days of John the Baptist "men of violence" were ready to take the kingdom by force (Matt. 11:12). Jesus' own disciples were caught up in that dream, eager to help God usher in the promises and to harness Jesus to their craving for glory.[21]

Priests and Pharisees regarded the promises of the kingdom a sheer fanaticism. They sent delegations to investigate John the Baptist and later Jesus.[22] They asked for some visible proof to authenticate Him and His message.[23] Everything had to be decided by their own sight and wisdom. If a visible sign were given, they would still be the judges of its adequacy. Jesus called them "an evil and adulterous [idolatrous] generation" (Matt. 16:4). The truth was that they did not want God to intrude or His kingdom to come. When the final invitation came, they rejected the very hope that had sustained Israel for generations. As the parable of excuses shows, they stumbled over God's invitation for the sake of enjoying a field just bought or five yoke of oxen or a new bride or their own "business." [24]

In Jesus Himself we see the striking alternative of "faith." What do you do when God has said, "You are my beloved Son," and yet after forty days in the dry wilderness there is no sign of confirmation, and nothing to eat but stones? You answer, "Man does not live by bread alone, but by every Word that proceeds out of the mouth of God." What do you do when the kingdom just does not arrive, when all experience testifies that God's promises are a fraud, when Satan mocks God by offering equivalent promises of his own in exchange for your worship? You answer, "You shall worship the Lord your God, and Him only shall you serve." You wait, trust God, and serve Him anyway (Matt. 4:1-11).

The stumbling blocks are very real. "The kingdom, the power, and the glory are what I seize and create," says the heart of the sinner. Against that arrogance stands the Word of God, the laughter of God, the wrath of God, the tears of God. There can be no compromise. Forgiveness, yes; but approval of lies, no.

A Lutheran education which teaches the Word of God "clearly and purely" will not obscure the stumbling block of the inheritance (kingdom), but will magnify it so that no hearer can evade it. A camel must become small enough to pass through the eye of a needle. The disciples were appalled. "Who then can be saved?" they asked. "With men, this is impossible," Jesus replied, "but with God all things are possible" (Matt. 19:23-26). Blessed are those pupils and teachers who experience the miracle, who become that small!

The Word of Servanthood as a Stumbling Block

In its third aspect God's Word calls upon us as sons and heirs of God to serve Him and one another. It is an obvious consequence. As His children, we do not have to expend anxiety and energy in discovering or proving who we are, or in gaining approval and avoiding accusation. As His heirs we do not have to devote our anxieties and energies toward creating our own life and future, as though our hope and joy depended upon fulfilling our own ambitions. We live by the promises of our Father who knows and unfolds every tomorrow to us, fills each day with His gifts, delivers us from evil, and preserves us for His kingdom and glory. We have no life to live, therefore, except that of being "about our Father's business" (Luke 2:49 AV). Our joy is to receive and use whatever gifts the Father invests in us, matching them to the opportunities and possibilities He unfolds to us. We imitate the Father's mercy, and delight in the wisdom of His commandments as we do them.

Here as always, Lutheran education looks to Jesus who has drawn us to Himself and made us in His and the Father's image. He wanted no life apart from that of doing His Father's will and work. He did not pursue wealth or delight in the praises of the crowds. He enjoyed the Father's simplest gifts. He did not cower before human threats, but walked steadfastly into risk and even death at His Father's call. The mountains would give way to Him, not He to them.[25] He was the instrument of the Father's mercy to sinners as He gathered the lost and scattered. People were never the enemy. This real enemy was sin, flesh, and the deceits of the devil. By these not only the Gentiles but also God's own people were held captive and were subject to the impending wrath of God.

Jesus served His Father by loving and praying even for a humanity which had turned altogether against Him. Gethsemane was His last chance to escape. He chose rather to drink the cup and to lay down His life for us. Trusting His Father's promises He took the lowest place and became the Servant of servants.[26] The promises did not fail. God highly exalted Him.[27] "Take up your cross and follow me," He now invites us (Matt. 16:24).

57

The stumbling block in that call to servanthood is readily apparent. Our natural flesh protests that God is asking too much, that He is projecting ideals which He surely does not expect us to take seriously. After all, says the flesh, we are "only human." To lose our life as Jesus did, to forfeit our rights, to become small in order that others may become great, to endure injustice meekly, to forgive those who oppress us, to see not people but the power of sin in them as the real enemy—all of this, in the judgment of our flesh, is a "yoke" too heavy to be borne (Matt. 11:29). God is too "hard" on us (Matt. 25:24). The flesh proposes that God make concessions and allow time off, so that we may "serve God *and* mammon" (Matt. 6:24). But it cannot work. Whenever the flesh survives, God gets only the external whitewash of a tomb whose inside is filled with death and all uncleanness.[28]

Jesus diagnoses the sin of Israel's leaders in the parable of the vineyard.[29] The tenants are supposed to be God's servants, but they have taken over God's church (the vineyard) as though it were their private possession. They see no need to listen to the messengers whose minority voices ask for God's true fruits. After all, they have power to kill even the "beloved son" and "heir" who conveys God's final appeal. Thereby they assert their own claim to be God's son and heir. "The inheritance will be ours," they say. But God will not allow them their victory. The very stone the builders rejected becomes the head of the corner.

Lutheran education needs to understand that the power of sin today has neither changed nor diminished from what it was then. The Word of life by which God calls His redeemed people to trust and serve Him in freedom becomes a stumbling block to their natural hearts. The church itself is readily deceived. It disguises its disobedience and distrust of God under a show of piety, clings to its tradition, exalts the authority of its leaders, justifies itself, shuts its ears to the Word, and imagines all is well. That is why "judgment" must always "begin with the household of God" (1 Pet. 4:17). That is why Jesus had to "save his people" including ourselves) from no other enemy than "their sins" (Matt. 1:18).

Let Lutheran education magnify and not minimize the stumbling block of the Word of servanthood! If God's Word encounters resistance, defensiveness, and even hatred, even so negative a reaction testifies that the Word is being taught "clearly and purely." That is how Lutheran education properly hallows God's name.

The Stumbling Block of the Cross

The drama of the stumbling block comes to its climactic focus in the hour of Jesus' crucifixion. Who is truly God's son? Who receives the inheritance? Who knows and trusts the Father and gives Him the uncompromising love of a whole heart? [30] Who loves his neighbor as himself and extends that love even to stranger and enemy? [31] Who manifests to the world the image of the Father's grace and truth? [32] In whom is the promised glory of the Lord revealed? [33]

The consistent answer is Jesus, Jesus only. The revelatory moment of that answer is the cross, that is, the history of Jesus' death and resurrection. In that hour Jesus is revealed as the only Son, the only Elect, the only Righteous, the only Heir, who by His own death gives life to the world. The cross is the sign of Jonah, the eye of the needle, the narrow gate, the only way to the Father, the blood that makes kosher. Every dimension of the stumbling block we have so far explored is comprehended in the cross.

The Scriptures know well what a stumbling block the cross is, but they offer no concessions.

> For Jews demand signs, and Greeks seek wisdom, but we preach Christ crucified, a stumbling block to Jews and folly to Gentiles, but to those who are called, both Jews and Greeks, Christ the power of God and the wisdom of God" (1 Cor. 1:22-24).

The cross is the death of Judaism. If Jesus is the only Son, then mere physical descent from Abraham and from the people brought out of Egypt no longer constitutes a claim on the sonship.[34] If election is in Christ, it is no longer in Abraham.[35] If Jesus' blood does the cleansing, all claims to be kosher by doing the works of the Law are done away.[36] Nowhere is the offense stated more graphically than in John 6:53 and context:

> Unless you eat the flesh of the Son of man and drink his blood, you have no life in you.

The crucified Jesus becomes the passover meal! We did it, now we must eat it; not to our eternal shame, but for forgiveness and eternal life. The stumbling block of that eating and drinking is staggering, however, for, in unity with baptism and the cross, it reduces fleshly circumcision to nothing.[37] Can the Jew possibly let go his whole heritage and piety "for the surpassing worth of knowing Jesus Christ" (Phil. 3:8)? Surely the old and familiar are good enough! Nicodemus protests, "How can a man be born again when he is old?" (John 3:4). The Law, fleshly genealogy, circumcision, these are Judaism's very "eye"! But Jesus does not yield:

> If your eye causes you to sin [becomes your stumbling block], pluck it out and throw it from you; it is better for you to enter life with one eye than with two eyes to be thrown into the hell of fire (Matt. 18:9).

To the Greek, on the other hand, the stumbling block in wisdom. The philosopher puts himself above the Word of the Cross, so that he may evaluate and control it. He decides that Jesus in His death is simply too small to fulfill the vision of a mightier one to come, or to be the glory of the Lord.[38] Is the world indeed to be judged by that one man whom God appointed "by raising him from the dead" (Acts 17:31)? That is too laughably narrow to be taken seriously! Either we know God everywhere, or we know Him nowhere! Thus "wisdom" to this day summons religions against God and the idolatry of human judgment against the truth of God.

An alternative tactic of wisdom is to reconstitute Jesus into something more palatably glorious and inoffensive. Magnify His deity and minimize the cross! Romanticize His birth and incarnation as though His glory were revealed in Christmas rather than in Good Friday and Easter. Marvel at His miraculous works and demonstrate that Christianity is still true by duplicating these works today. Think of Jesus as the glorious God against whom Satan's temptations are a futile enterprise, who would not really have needed to pray to God as His "Father," whose glory is revealed not in the weakness of His love and death but in the power of His deeds and resurrection. Of course we cannot really follow Jesus then, for we are "only human," and He is not quite one of us after all! So says our "wisdom."

Or else "wisdom" will heighten the *mystery* of Christ. In place of faith in His blood, substitute a feeling of awe in the presence of holiness. Then the stumbling block is transcended and "the cross of Christ [is] emptied of its power" (1 Cor. 1:17). Thus "wisdom" seeks a Gospel of which it need not be "ashamed" (Rom. 1:16).

By way of the Lord's purifying, Lutheran education will know how to direct the Word of God ever more clearly to the heart of the sinner, namely, by magnifying the stumbling block of the cross. For the sign of the cross is not a pious religious symbol to be stroked fleetingly in the air. It is rather the very beginning and foundation of life to us, as Paul says,

> But far be it from me to glory except in the cross of our Lord Jesus Christ, by which the world has been crucified to me and I to the world. . . . Peace and mercy be upon all who walk by this rule, upon the Israel of God (Gal. 6:15-16).

INAUTHENTIC STUMBLING BLOCKS AND A FALSE FAITH

As we magnify the offensiveness of the Word of God and of the cross of Christ, we come to understand why our natural hearts resist and even hate that Word. The miracle of faith becomes the more astounding to us then. We recognize how the Spirit through the Word must actually put our old flesh to death, so as to raise us up to His new life of joy and freedom in Christ.

There is an additional benefit for us, however, in understanding the true stumbling block. By that understanding we are the better equipped to detect and to avoid inauthentic stumbling blocks which the guile of the devil sets in our way. The imagery of the stumbling block converges at this point with that of the combination lock in our previous chapter. If false stumbling blocks are set in our way, they trip us up and divert us from the path of the Lord's life. If false or uncertain stopping points are imposed on the combination dial, the lock does not spring open and the prisoner is not freed. The cause of unbelief in that case does not lie in the natural ungodliness and pride of the sinner's heart. He has not even encountered the authentic stone of stumbling and rock of offense. Something else tripped him up. The Word which purported to be God's was not taught clearly and purely, but obscured by impurities.

Thus we return to the imagery of the purifying. If there were no impurity among and within us, there would be no need for the Lord's fire. As it is, the very existence of our fiery conflict testifies that there must be a dross mingled with our gold, false stopping points on our combination dial, inauthentic stumbling blocks to make us fall.

Our true gold is the Gospel of the cross which we have unfolded

61

from the Scriptures at considerable length. By this Word, Christ receives His true honor as our only Savior, and our terrified hearts experience rest and comfort in Him alone. By this Word our gracious Father exalts us to be His children and heirs with Christ, promises to be our God, and invites us to serve Him and to love one another. This is the Holy Spirit's Word, sealed and testified also in the sacraments. Its effect is faith, a clean heart and a right spirit within us, a new life, and the gathering of the Church into one Body as Christ's holy people. This Gospel is and has always been Lutheran education's treasure and power. It is the glory of our Synod's doctrinal position. The grace of God has preserved it to us, so that to this day we delight to teach and proclaim it. This Word is our Rock. It holds us firm and unshaken against every threat and fear, so that we dare to walk with our Lord even through His fire. It is our authentic gold. By it we ourselves are pure gold in God's sight.

Mingled with our gold, however, there is also a dross. The dross is *not* the use of the historical-critical method in Bible study, as we had first thought. That method of itself is quite external to our doctrine, as we shall see in the next chapter. The real dross lies *within* our doctrine. It is mixed and fused with what we have called "Synod's doctrinal position." That is why the fire is so painful for us, and so incomprehensible. We have believed, and Lutheran education has played a role in assuring us, that our Synod possesses the *pure* doctrine. We could therefore measure the doctrine of other churches by our own, without ever suspecting that our own might need serious testing. Whatever our Synod taught, we assumed, must surely be "Scriptural and Confessional." Our recently adopted "Statement" implies as much in its very title. But what if the impurity our Lord intends to purge is inherent in the very "doctrinal position" we are determined must not be changed? If His fire begins to expose that possibility to us, dare we resist its pain? Must we not rather praise God for His mercy, trust Him to do what He has in mind, and plead with Him to finish it quickly?

The dross, as we have suggested, is rooted in a confusion regarding the term "the Word of God." In Biblical usage and in Luther's Small Catechism, God's Word means essentially the Gospel, conveyed to us in the form of words, by which the Holy Spirit draws us to the Father through Christ and makes us His own. In the prevailing theology of our Synod, however, the Word of God is taken to mean the Holy Scriptures. And Scripture is the Word of God, not because its Gospel is the Word of God, but because God is the true author of every word of the Bible. Anything less is rejected as "Gospel reductionism." Indeed, if the entire Holy Scripture is not pure and inerrant gold by virtue of its inspired authorship, then even its Gospel ceases to be gold.

This is the rationale of the dross. It follows that critical study of the Bible is the great enemy. People who use or condone the historical-critical method do not respect the essential goldness of the Scriptures, namely, their plenary inspiration, inerrancy, and authority as God's divinely authored Word. The issue in Synod's controversy, the dross insists, is not the Gospel. It is rather the goldness of the inspired Bible.

To the dross the Scriptures are gold in their own right, quite apart from the gold of their Gospel. Inevitably, then, the Scriptures are regarded as broader than the Gospel. Beyond their content of Law and Gospel there remains "the rest of Scripture." The Scriptures contain also "information about other matters." [39] Christians must also "accept matters taught in the Scriptures which are not a part of the Gospel." [40] Thus, in the mind of the dross, the message which Christians must accept to be true Christians, is *more* than Christ alone! It is *more* than "the Gospel of the gracious justification of the sinner through faith in Jesus Christ." [41] "Anything and everything that the Scriptures teach" now belongs to our Synod's faith and confession.[42]

In defining all this as "dross" and distinguishing it from our gold, we are sharing an insight to which the Lord's purifying fire has driven us personally. We have no authority to impose our judgment on any reader, however, and desire none. The cleansing must finally be the Lord's work, will, and wisdom, not ours or any man's. What matters now is not who among us is right or wrong. Our Lord makes use of wrongness as well as of rightness to expose what must be exposed and to finish His work. If anyone has been wrong, God's grace toward him is not diminished but abounds all the more. If anyone's insight stands the test and proves right, God does not love him the more for his rightness. What matters is only that He use any of us in any way He pleases toward exposing and purging out our dross, so that His gold may shine among and through us in its full purity.

The foremost question, therefore, is not how much pain any of us may suffer, whether from outside or from within ourselves. The question is not what will become of our beloved Synod. Such questions we can gladly trust to our Lord. For us as Lutheran teachers and pastors the vital questions are those which affect our hearers. Are we putting alien stumbling blocks in the way of our little ones? Are we using the Word of God in such a way that the captives of sin are truly being set free? Are we imposing burdens of man-made laws "hard to bear," and lifting them with not so much as a finger (Matt. 23:4)? Are we ourselves so filled with the joy and freedom of the Word of life, that we cannot wait to pour out more of its treasures to anyone who will only hear?

Jesus' Conflict with Inauthentic Stumbling Blocks—and Ours

The purifying fire that raged against the dross in Jesus' day serves to illuminate the fire we are experiencing. It was not difficult for the leaders of Judaism to "deceive the hearts of the simple" by words which seemed "fair and flattering," as Paul puts it in Rom. 16:18. To be sure, the rulers themselves did not know what they were doing, as Jesus acknowledges also when He refers to them as blind.[43] They thought they were acting responsibly before God to resolve confusions Jesus had caused and to restore the people to the discipline of their law. Yet the forces they summoned were the very ones which are working in our own church.

There was *tradition,* meaning "the way I was brought up, the way I was always taught." Whether in our Synod or in Judaism, education is always the instrument of tradition. It does not readily occur to devout people that the tradition they learned can err. That is why dross is able to mingle undetected with truth, as though it were truth. The dross may then even become a ground of comfort and stability, until it emerges finally as the unchallenged measure of everything else. That is why every true prophet, standing by necessity against dross, has found himself to be an accused and persecuted minority.[44]

When the Jews challenged Jesus with the question: "Are you greater than our father Abraham? Who do you think you are?" (John 8:53) they were in effect appealing to their tradition. Today someone might argue, "Do you think you are greater than Walther?" The Pharisees could invoke the piety of the kosher and point to Jesus' obvious violations of it, much as we today invoke "the doctrinal position of Synod." Anybody who brings in something "new" or questions the traditional concept of doctrine at any point is immediately under suspicion. Familiar forms of thought provide stability. Change introduces uncertainty and is viewed as a great threat.

Similarly the dross is able to invoke the *authority of leaders*. By God's own governance even a humanity which does not know Him is conditioned to respect structured authority and to find stability in it. Such respect transfers readily to the structured government of the church. In Jesus' day the people relied on the authority of scribe and synagogue, of priest and temple. They did not easily catch the distinction (and neither do we) between the kind of authority implicit in any position of institutional responsibility and the altogether unique authority inherent in the proclaiming of God's Word.

Hence it seemed perfectly in order that Judaism's institutional authorities (the chief priests and elders) should ask Jesus, "Where is *your* authority? Who gave it to you?" (Matt. 21:23). If Jesus claimed to have authority from God, He was expected to demonstrate it with a sign from heaven. Neither the people nor their leaders understood that a prophet's true authority lies simply in the Word which God has sent him to proclaim. By listening to his Word the hearers will discover and know the prophet's authority. Indeed, that alone explains how the people had come to "hold that John the Baptist was a prophet" (Matt. 21:27). Judaism's leaders, however, could think of authority only in terms of institutionalized credentials. If Jesus lacks official certification, He has no authority to speak or act in the name of God. Nobody need listen to Him. If the authorized religious leaders then tell Him to keep silent and He does not, He is a disobedient rebel, an individualist who thinks He can impose His private notions on the whole people and has to listen to nobody!

What a masterful trap the dross is able to set, once it has obscured the authority inherent in the Gospel! [45] We ourselves are in no way immune to the danger. Without realizing it, we may come to rely on the visible, concrete, official, and structured authority of the synodical institution. The authority of the Synod in convention, of adopted resolutions, of duly elected officials, and of the constitution, becomes for us the instrument of the church's stability. In our grave difficulty and division we look to these authorities to establish truth, restore unity and peace, keep order, and deal with rebellion by firm discipline. Behind such institutional authority the dross hides itself, rejecting and silencing any word or insight that might begin to expose it. "Peace, peace," the dross promises. "But there is no peace," says the Lord (Jer. 8:11).

Thus the dross sets *tradition* and institutional *authority* as stumbling blocks to trip us up, so that we fail to look to the glory of God in the face of Christ alone. But the dross is still not satisfied. It adds still another stumbling block, *the Scriptures!*

It is an incredible tactic. Once again the conflict between Jesus and Pharisaism enables us to see how the dross accomplishes it. The rulers of synagogue and temple did not claim to have authority simply by virtue of their public office. They invoked "Moses and the prophets," just as we invoke the Scriptures. "Moses" was their sacred foundation, the source and proof of everything they taught concerning the law and the character of God's chosen people. Nevertheless the Scriptures became a focal point of the conflict between them and Jesus. Jesus charged that they were not really *hearing* the Scriptures for what God was really saying. They were only *claiming* Moses as authority for their *tradition*. Jesus called their tradition and doctrine "commandments of men." Although it presented itself as "the Word of God," its effect was "to make void the word of God" (Matt. 15:6). Because of the tradition, the people were kept from hearing what God was really saying to them in Moses and in the Scriptures.

The drama unfolds in many of Jesus' sayings. "They *have* Moses and the prophets," Abraham says to the rich man, "Let them *hear* them" (Luke 16:29). It is not enough that the seed of the Word of God is sown, Jesus says. "He who has ears, let him *hear*" (Luke 8:8). If, instead of merely glorifying the Scriptures as the source of eternal life you would actually *search* what they are saying, Jesus pleads, you would discover that "they bear witness to me" (John 5:39)! For the Scriptures say exactly what Jesus is saying, and call God's people to serve and trust God exactly the way Jesus serves and trusts Him. But if they will not hear the Scriptures, then

> Do not think that it is I who shall accuse you to the Father; it is Moses who accuses you, on whom you set your hope. If you believed Moses, you would believe me, for he wrote of me. But if

you do not believe his writings, how will you believe my words? (John 5:45-47)

We can see then how the dross manages to turn even the Scriptures into a stumbling block. First it inculcates the highest respect and reverence for the Scriptures. Then it harnesses that reverence simply to confirm the tradition in which the people were brought up. Thus "Moses" and the "tradition" become the same thing. The Scriptures are not used to put the tradition to the test. They are allowed to say or mean only what the scribes say they mean. The Word of God in Scripture is not searched or heard. The Bible is highly revered, but it becomes a closed book.

The parallel to our own situation seems painfully close. We find ourselves doing battle to uphold the authority of the Scriptures as the inspired Word of God. This authority principle, the dross argues, is the root presupposition by which we must approach the Scriptures. Once this presupposition is accepted we may open the Bible anywhere and know that what we read is without question God's own Word. Thus if the authority of the Bible itself has been firmly established, then everything in the Scriptures will be accepted out of reverence for that authority.

But is that the way the Spirit and faith work? When Jesus Himself read the Scriptures, He searched to hear what God was saying to Him. Its words came to life by the Spirit. They were not "letter" (2 Cor. 3:6) made sacred by the mere sacredness of the holy scroll. The words had content! They were "filled full" of meaning and truth (that is what "fulfilled" means!), so that Jesus in turn "fulfilled" the Scriptures by His very life of trust and obedience and joy in His Father. The same Spirit who had filled the prophets in the first place now filled Jesus through their words. That is why the people were astonished at Jesus' preaching. They detected something unique. "He taught them as one who *had authority,* and not as the scribes" (Matt. 7:29).

Hence the proper presupposition by which we are to approach the Scriptures is simply the expectation of faith in Christ that they will indeed speak to us, and that Christ will open the Scriptures to us as He did to His disciples.[46] But if the dross prevails, the Scriptures become a stumbling block in our path. No longer is it the doctrine of justification by grace, for Christ's sake, through faith that "opens the door to the entire Bible," as our Confessions declare.[47] The door to the Bible is rather the presupposition that all the information it offers is true and inerrant, of which Christ is only a part. Thereby the Bible rules over the Gospel. The glory of the doctrine of inspiration prevails over the glory of the cross.

The dross's final stumbling block is *repression*. Jesus experienced it. The leaders of Judaism were sure they were right and Jesus was wrong. They listened not to hear what He was saying, but to find some ground on which to accuse Him.[48] At His trial they were disconcerted when no charge against Him would really stick, but only momentarily. Caiaphas resolved the matter by getting Jesus to confess in the presence of them all that He was the Son of God. By their understanding of doctrinal truth that was blasphemy.[49] And so they were rid of Him, and able to return to their normal and well controlled religious routine.

The dross always presents itself as the perfection of divine truth. It follows that whatever challenges the dross must be untruth. The way to deal with untruth is to suppress it, so that the people will not be confused or disturbed by it. If its dissemination cannot be wholly prevented, the minds of the people must at least be conditioned to assume in advance that any challenging argument is in error, that its author is guilty of false doctrine, and that hearing him is a waste of effort. The dross does not encourage people to think or to raise questions. To question Scripture or the true doctrine at any point is to doubt, and doubt is the beginning of unbelief. From our own childhood and youth we recall being exhorted with all earnestness: "We do not question the Word of God!" Or, "You don't have to understand it, just believe it!" Or, "You should not ask that!" Thinking was subtly discouraged as a kind of impiety and a danger to the soul.

It follows also that the varied gifts which the Spirit invests in various members of Christ's Body are not so much welcomed as feared. Varied backgrounds and insights threaten the unity of the doctrine and of the Body. If everyone is free to express his individualistic ideas, the church will be unduly disturbed. Besides, mistakenness cannot be permitted. Therefore it seems wise to protect the true doctrine by submitting all theological writings to "doctrinal review" before publication. If members of the church dissent from any doctrinal resolution of the Synod, their dissent should be processed through orderly institutional channels. Then the people will not have to hear of it or be disturbed by it.

Thus the dross secures itself against any serious testing or close examination. If anyone is bold enough to challenge the dross publicly, he will be accused of disturbing the church and of trying to undermine the true doctrine. Therefore even those who do sense some problem in the church's doctrine are careful about expressing what they really see. To expose their ideas to public view is not only futile but may well be personally disastrous. We marvel the more, therefore, when we see Jesus declaring that He *must* go to Jerusalem to confront the highest authorities in the very precincts of the holy temple, while knowing full well that they will only revile Him and put Him to death.[50] We begin to understand also the context of oppression which leads Jesus to tell His disciples:

> So have no fear of them. For nothing is covered that will not be revealed, or hidden that will not be known. What I tell you in the dark, utter in the light; and what you hear whispered, proclaim upon the housetops. And do not fear those who kill the body but cannot kill the soul (Matt. 10:26-28).

The climate of fear in our church is pervasive and of long standing. In 1959 the President of Synod asked my father to write a monograph on the doctrine of the Scriptures. He declined. Only in private did he confide his real reason: "What needs to be said, the Missouri Synod cannot hear." He understood well the forces of repression at work in our church. If what he wrote were to depart at all from the Synod's traditional form of doctrine, it would not gain a hearing. The Synod would simply not publish it. But if it did, or if he published it independently, he would only subject himself to personal accusation and recrimination. Thus repression is the final stumbling block by which the dross preserves itself from discovery.

It is different now. The day of reckoning has come. The Lord's fire is upon us.

Footnotes for Chapter III

[1] Thesis 62 of the "Ninety-five Theses," *Luther's Works* (Philadelphia: Muhlenberg Press, 1957), vol. 31, p. 31.
[2] Rom. 8:7-8.
[3] Is. 6:9-10; John 12:39-42; Acts 28:26-27.
[4] Is. 6:9-10; 8:14.

[5] 1 Pet. 2:6-8; Luke 20:17-18.
[6] See Rom. 9:32-33; 11:9.
[7] Rom. 14:13.
[8] 1 Cor. 1:23; Gal. 5:11.
[9] Is. 40:2.
[10] Rom. 8:33-34; John 10:28-29.
[11] Ps. 113:7; Ezek. 16:1-14; 1 Tim. 1:15.
[12] Luke 14:7-11.
[13] Luke 18:9–14.
[14] Mark 2:7.
[15] Luke 7:29-30.
[16] Matt. 9:2-3,10-13; Luke 15:1; 19:7.
[17] Luke 15:11-32.
[18] John 8:48; 9:24; 10:30-33.
[19] John 8:42-47.
[20] Ps. 16:5-11; Hos. 6:2-3; John 11:25-26; Rom. 8:37-39.
[21] Matt. 20:20-21; Luke 9:54.
[22] Matt. 3:6; 15:1.
[23] Matt. 12:38; 16:1.
[24] Luke 14:15-24; Matt. 22:5.
[25] Matt. 21:21; Ps. 46:2-3.
[26] Matt. 20:25–28.
[27] Phil. 2:4-11.
[28] Matt. 23:25-28.
[29] Mark 12:1-11.
[30] Deut. 6:4-5; Mark 12:29-31.
[31] Lev. 19:18,34; Luke 10:25-37.
[32] John 1:17-18; Ps. 100:5.
[33] Is. 40:5; 60:1-3; Luke 3:4-6; John 1:14.
[34] Ex. 4:22-23; Matt. 3:9; John 8:39-40,56-58.
[35] Eph. 1:3-14; Luke 16:22-30; Gal. 3:25-29.
[36] 1 John 1:7; Heb. 9:12-15.
[37] John 6:60-61; Gal. 3:27; 6:12-17.
[38] Is. 40:5; Matt. 3:11.
[39] "Gospel and Scripture: The Interrelationship of the Material and Formal Principles in Lutheran Theology," A Report of the Commission on Theology and Church Relations, The Lutheran Church—Missouri Synod, November, 1972, pp. 10, 12.
[40] "A Statement of Scriptural and Confessional Principles," IV,C,4.
[41] *Ibid.,* IV,C.
[42] *Ibid.,* Conclusion.
[43] Matt. 15:14; Luke 23:34; Acts 3:17.
[44] Matt. 21:34-39; 22:6; 23:29-37.
[45] On the authority question see also John 8:31-32,47; 1 Cor. 2:1-5; 2 Cor. 2:14-3:6; 1 Thess. 2:13.
[46] Luke 24:27,32,44-45.
[47] Apology IV,2 (German). Quoted in "Gospel and Scripture," p. 6.
[48] Luke 19:47-48; 20:20,26.
[49] Matt. 26:59-66.
[50] Matt. 16:21.

Chapter IV

The Use of Scripture in Lutheran Education

As the Lord's fire purifies our gold and separates out the dross, Lutheran education will surely emerge with an enriched joy and confidence in the Holy Scriptures. We shall know what the authority of Scripture really is and what it means to submit to that authority. Thereby we shall also know more clearly how the Holy Scriptures are to be used.

LEAVING THE DROSS BEHIND

The authority of Scripture consists in nothing else than the authority of our Lord Jesus Christ inherent in the golden Gospel which proclaims Him to our hearts. Once the dross is left behind, that authority will be Lutheran education's single presupposition for the study of the Bible. We know the God, the Christ, and the Spirit of the Scriptures. We therefore approach the Scriptures in the expectation that they will enrich us further in our knowledge of God. We expect that the Scriptures will magnify Christ to us in all His uniqueness as God's only Son, and draw us to the Father through Him. We expect also that the Scriptures as our only rule and norm will purify our knowledge of God against all subtle accretions of fleshly wisdom and dross. We know in advance that the Scriptures are of God. Therefore nothing any interpreter finds or thinks he finds will ever erase Christ from the Scriptures, or negate the Scriptures as the Word of God. For the truth of the Scriptures does not depend upon the processes and insights of men who try to understand them, but upon God and His unfailing promises.

It is good and right, therefore, and not at all a threat to the Scriptures, that God's holy people use every gift of keen thinking and special training with which God has equipped any of them. For the Scriptures are no casual curiosity. They ask us to search them closely. They challenge us to discover and explore every possible question. The effort to understand them and to make the fullest sense out of every historical or literary perplexity in no way contradicts our con-

73

fidence in the Scriptures as the Word of God. Lutheran education will not burden interpreters of Scripture with the impossible demand that they be absolutely and eternally right in every conclusion they express. Our eternal rightness before God does not consist in the perfection of our works after all, but solely in God's sustaining love in Christ our Lord. Therefore the struggle against the inadequacies of human understanding goes on continually. We use our minds then not only to understand the Scriptures, but also to learn from and to test one another.

What really matters is only this, that as we approach the study of the Scriptures we know Christ our Lord and rest in Him. By that faith and confidence we shall be taking "every thought captive to obey Christ," as Paul puts it (2 Cor. 10:5). Our captivity to Christ not only *sets us free* to think, but actually *summons us* to think as clearly as we can. It requires us to yield to what makes the clearest sense in terms of the evidence, without fearing the consequences!

The dross which has so plagued us comprehends none of these things. The dross does not understand what such captivity to Christ means, nor what freedom in Christ means, nor what it means to invest our full talents without fear at His command. By the fallacy of the dross, as we have seen, "the Word of God" does not mean simply what God is telling us of Christ through the Gospel and the Scriptures. Our dross has diverted us from this "gold," and enticed us to magnify the Scriptures themselves, even apart from their Gospel, as "the Word of God." The dross thinks that the Bible's "inspiration" means its *divine authorship*!

From that point on, the rationale of the dross entangles us step by step. "The Word of God" calls for faith and obedience, the dross argues (and no child of God could possibly disagree with that). For the dross, however, it follows that our faith and obedience must then be directed *not to Christ through the Gospel, but to the Scriptures*! The dross argues that we must "sacrifice our intellect," that we must believe "in what the natural reason of man considers absurd," that we must "take our minds and thoughts captive to the Scriptures." [1] Notice the dramatic shift! Our thoughts are not "captive to obey *Christ*" (2 Cor. 10:5) whom the Scriptures proclaim. The dross commands rather that our thoughts *obey the Scriptures* as a divinely authored book!

74

The next step in the logic of the dross is that the church must rally to save the authority of the Scriptures from those who appear to be its detractors. In so doing the church must establish the correct interpretation of disputed texts, decisively and authoritatively, by taking a vote on the matter at a convention.[2] Trapped by its dross, the church then knows no alternative but to be firm and uncompromising in enforcing conformity to its decreed truth. It must harness the power of institutional discipline to compel dissidents to yield and behave or to get out. The unity of one faith in one Christ which the Scriptures themselves proclaim [3] now gives way to another concept of unity. Unity means walking together as a Synod, and walking together means agreeing peaceably to interpretations adopted by majority rule.

The most vital question, however, is not what such fallacious reasoning is doing to our Synod, but what it is doing to souls. "No other foundation can any man lay than that which is laid, which is Jesus Christ," Paul declares (1 Cor. 3:11). Nevertheless by our dross we have been pointing our people to an "other foundation," quite distinct from Paul's. In a recent document issued by our Synod, our "foundation" is explicitly affirmed to be *the Scriptures,* and that without any reference to Christ whatsoever! Three venerable fathers of our church are cited:

> Our church has taken for *the foundation on which she stands* the Holy Scriptures, and on it she stands honestly and squarely; from *this foundation* she will not depart one finger's breadth (Walther, *Lehre und Wehre,* 1971, p. 11). (Our emphasis)

Again:

> The Church of the Reformation stands on the rock of Holy Scripture, on the *Sola Scriptura* (Pieper, *Lehre und Wehre,* 1928, p. 14).

And yet again:

> The *entire theological edifice is undermined* and hollowed out if it is no longer *borne by* the inspired, infallible Word of Scripture. . . . If the Bible is no longer the infallible Word of God but a human, fallible record of the things of which it treats, the . . . [classical proof passages for a position or doctrine] are no longer of any avail. A veritable deluge of all manner of skeptical questions concerning the origin and content of Scripture is unloosed which cannot be checked and controlled (Bente, *Lehre und Wehre,* 1902, p. 130).[4] (Our emphasis)

The honored fathers here quoted were not aware of the dross which the Lord's fire is only now exposing to our generation. In any case their understandings do not constitute our Synod's "rule and norm."

We cannot evade the question *what is really our foundation?* We sing joyfully, "The church's one foundation is Jesus Christ her Lord." In another hymn we confess that we "stand" on Christ alone as "our solid rock," and that "all other ground is sinking sand." [5] What is our foundation and rock then? Is it really Christ alone? Or is it, in Bente's phrase, "the inspired infallible Word of Scripture"? Does our Synod mean to say that Christ and the Scriptures are in reality one and the same foundation? If so, why has it repudiated this very definition of the authority of Scripture as "Gospel reductionism"? [6] It would appear that our Synod wishes to regard Scripture as a *foundation* distinct and different from merely Christ and the Gospel! It wants us to stand on *two* foundations.

How, then, are these two foundations related? Is Christ a sub-foundation under the Scriptures? Are the Scriptures a sub-foundation under the Gospel? Was Christ the foundation only in apostolic times (when the New Testament was not yet written), whereas Scripture is now the foundation *for us?* [7] Or do we set our two foundations side by side, like two rocks, planting one foot upon each? But that is the kind of ambiguity the Lord found intolerable when Elijah said, "How long will you go limping with two opinions?" (1 Kings 18:21), and again when Jesus said, "No man can serve two masters" (Matt. 6:24). The Lord's fire has forced this question upon us, and He demands that we face it! [8]

For the common piety of our people this unnoticed mixture of dross with our gold has been devastating. By our dross we confused "believing in Christ" with "believing in the Bible," as though these were the same thing. For many, "believing *the Bible* from cover to cover" became the touchstone of "evangelical" Christianity over against liberalism, with no awareness that "evangelical" means *Gospel!* By our dross Christ and the Gospel were set aside as "not the issue" in our controversy, but a distraction. The *real* issue, we were told, was that of "Bible believers" over against "Bible doubters." Thus faith and unbelief were made to turn, not on what men think of *Christ,* [9] but on what they think of *the Bible.* By our dross the slogan "They are taking our Bible away from us" was able to generate fear, anger, and a dedicated zeal to do what we somehow could not quite trust God to do, namely, save His Bible. By our dross we called "evil good and good evil"; we "put darkness for light and light for darkness" (Is. 5:20). The dross has been destroying us. But now the dross itself will be destroyed. The Lord's fire will tolerate it no longer.

With the purging of the dross Lutheran education, together with the whole church, stands on the borders of a promised but unexplored land. "You have not passed this way before," Joshua would acknowledge to us as he did to Israel of old (Josh. 3:3-4). A whole new world of Biblical understanding and of insight into the Gospel lies before us, like a land flowing with milk and honey. The prospect is simultaneously exciting and fearsome. We dare venture forward as Joshua did, only by following the Lord of the New Covenant as He leads us into territories the dross has forbidden. The challenge of Caleb offers us a lively encouragement:

> If the Lord delights in us, He will bring us into this land and give it to us. Only, do not rebel against the Lord (Num. 14:8-9).

But if the dross still generates a throwing of stones, there is precedent for that too.[10]

Historicity, Facticity, and the Rest of Scripture

When the dross has been left behind, Lutheran education will hold to "the Word of God" in a single meaning of that phrase. The Word of God is the message, formulated in human words, which God addresses to our hearts out of the cross of Christ. Its closest synonym would be the term "Gospel," [11] whether in the narrow focus of absolution (the pronouncement of forgiveness), or in a wider sense that takes in all articles of Christian confession, or in the widest sense that includes also God's Word of Law and wrath. Scripture is properly called "the Word of God," then, for the sake of the Gospel of truth and life in Christ which is its glory. Because of this message the Scriptures are our pure and clear fountain and our only rule and norm for faith and life.

Not all questions pertaining to Lutheran education's use of the Scriptures are answered, however, simply by leaving the dross behind. If the Scriptures are to be understood as "the Word of God" for the sake of its Gospel, what is the status of "the rest of Scripture," or of that Biblical content which is "not a part of the Gospel"? What becomes of the "historicity and facticity" of Biblical narratives? Can there be a Gospel without the events which that very Gospel proclaims? Such questions are not only inevitable but valuable and necessary. Lutheran education cannot properly use the Scriptures unless it has come to terms with them.

One possibility looms immediately. If the truth and authority of Holy Scripture is defined in terms of the Gospel, it seems to follow that the Bible is being divided into "parts." The Gospel is then only one *part* of Scripture. The other *part* is the leftovers. We conjure the image of some "editor" who will undertake to sort out these two parts. He may then issue an edition of the Bible in which "the Gospel part" is printed in red, and "the rest" in black. Perhaps abbreviated Bibles would appear, which would include only "the Gospel part" and omit "the rest." Simply to propose such a possibility is already to realize how superficial, artificial, and even stupid it would be. If the Scriptures are thought of in terms of such "parts," they cease to be the Scriptures God has given us and which we have cherished as "the Word of God." There has to be a better answer than that.

And there is. Once the dross with its suspicions and fears is out of the way, a much simpler possibility offers itself. We are not dealing with two "parts" of the Bible at all, but with two pervasive "realities." If the Bible is to be known and treasured for what it truly is, these two realities must be taken into account simultaneously and at all times. We shall call the one reality "theological" (of God) and the other "historical" (of men). The *theological* reality may be diagrammed as a vertical line descending from heaven to earth This line, marked by the cross, bears the Word of Christ to our hearts as from God Himself through the Spirit. The *historical* reality we would then diagram as a horizontal line. We ourselves, as people within the whole of flesh and blood humanity, belong to this horizontal. Our personal historicity is not different in kind from the historicity of our forefathers who wrote the Bible, who heard and read its message in each original setting and occasion, or about whom the Scriptures speak.

The two lines intersect. The vertical cuts through the horizontal, both within the Scriptures and within ourselves, whenever and wherever the Word of God is spoken and heard by human beings. At the point of the intersecting, the "sparks" of the Spirit's power fly, as it were. We experience that power wherever that Word of the Gospel, through preaching, teaching, sacrament, or the Scriptures themselves, bursts into Spirit and life for us. The diagram at the beginning of this chapter attempts to visualize these two intersecting realities of the Holy Scriptures.[12]

It is immediately evident that what we call the "historical reality" of Scripture is not only precious but indispensable. Without it the "theological reality," the vertical "Word of God" would be inexpressible, unknowable, and unknown. For the Word of God does not float about as some kind of vague abstraction or mystical feeling. It takes form in human words, so that by such words it may continue to pierce hearts,[13] break rocks in pieces,[14] and penetrate our own actual humanity and experience. We search the Scriptures to understand how the Word of God broke through to transform people like ourselves, whose hearts God fashioned just like our own,[15] so that the same Word of God may do its holy work also in us. As the vertical breaks through the human history to which we ourselves belong, texts come to life. Human words on humanly inscribed pages yield a truth which "no eye has seen, nor ear heard, nor the heart of man conceived" (1 Cor. 2:9). A text which seemed to us to be simply holy words, and which we thought we understood, is "fulfilled (filled full) in our hearing," even today (Luke 4:21). Therefore Lutheran education, in teaching the Scriptures, will unfold clearly and at every opportunity the intersecting of God's Word with our history. Every new discovery of such intersecting will only confirm and vindicate our confidence that the Scriptures are indeed "the written Word of God"; and not only certain "parts" of Scripture, but the whole precious Book as God has given and preserved it for us to this day.

Two possible alternatives to our concept of intersecting "realities" of Scripture suggest themselves. Lutheran education will need to be aware of them, so as to put these as well as our own proposal to the test. The first alternative would be to lay also our vertical line horizontal. In that case what we call Scripture's "theological reality" would run *parallel* to the "historical," rather than intersect it. This alternative would represent the approach of people who do not expect to hear God speak to them in the Scriptures. Even texts which bring to us the most obvious and vivid comfort are reduced to merely human ideas out of past religious speculation. The Bible then is in no sense the Word of God. The Christian faith itself becomes only a passing episode in the history of religions. The glory of Scripture remains totally unrecognized and unknown.

The second alternative would be to turn the historical reality of Scripture vertical rather than horizontal. The historical reality would then run parallel to, or perhaps even be identified with, the theological reality of the Scriptures. Here again, the intersecting force of the Word of God would be obscured and unrecognized. This alternative to our diagram represents, we suggest, what the dross has done to our church. We are compelled now to envision Scripture as having "parts." The Gospel (our vertical line) is only one part. The rest of Scripture (our horizontal reality now turned vertical) becomes another part. This other part is in itself the Word of God, equally with and in the same way as the Gospel. To say otherwise is to limit the Bible's divine authority and the scope of its inspiration. Hence the "historicity" of events recorded in Scripture turns out to be different in kind from our own historicity. Biblical historicity is then something unique. Its truth is guaranteed by divine inspiration. It cannot be searched, tested, or tampered with by human historical thinking. That would be to impose man's reason over the Word of God and to subject the holy historicity of the Bible to human skepticism and unbelief.

Although this argumentation is intended to preserve the authority of the Bible, its effect is to obscure and confuse the Scriptures in terms of both "realities." The vertical reality is obscured because something else and more than the Gospel must now be believed as the Word of God. The horizontal reality is obscured because the Bible is not trusted to be genuinely historical and part of our own human historicity. It is separated from us, and made so divine that we cannot really search to know it. For example, the disciples of Jesus are called to "witness" to what they themselves "saw and heard" as part of their own human history and experience.[16] We are not allowed to ask them questions, however, or to press their human testimony in any way. Our own humanness is excluded as a resource for understanding theirs. Hence we cannot get at even the most vital "historical-theological" question, namely, how it came about that in

Jesus' death and resurrection the Word of God broke through to transform the disciples so radically, and to raise them up from death to life.

Our proposal that Scripture be understood in terms of two inter secting "realities" rather than in terms of "parts" is offered as a step toward clarifications which are vitally needed. Assuming for the moment that this approach is not without merit, what might its consequences be for Lutheran education in its use of the Scriptures?

SCRIPTURE AS THE WORD OF GOD
(THEOLOGICAL REALITY)

What we call the "theological reality" of Scripture is actually experienced by anyone who reads his Bible with a heart that asks, seeks, and knocks according to Christ's promise.[17] Inadequate understanding and unanswered questions cannot inhibit the cumulative delight of discovery. Words come to life in hearts that hunger for comfort. A little insight one day sparks another insight the next. Though the reading and pondering continues for a lifetime, the riches of newness are inexhaustible.

It is a precious experience for two Christians who love the Scriptures to compare the markings their Bibles have accumulated over an extended period of time. The markings tend to cluster. Such clustering suggests that in certain sections "the Word of God" reaches hearts very readily with its comfort and wisdom. It does not take much in the way of "interpreting" for the Spirit's power to break through. The hungry heart is fed. The Word of God comes to life off the printed page and penetrates like a voice from heaven!

This experience of printed words, suddenly "filled" with lively content and personal meaning, corresponds to what saints of God within the New Testament experienced when they used the word "fulfilled." Words long known on manuscript and scroll really speak! By those words God's own truth and presence enter into what His people are experiencing and suffering. God's hand is visible. His promise becomes the very definition of life. The evident forces of sin and accusation, of disaster and death, no longer have the last word. Great riches wait to be mined when the "fulfilled" texts are searched in this sight. We need to recover more fully how the Scriptures brought life and power to Jesus or to the Apostles who quoted them. Yet what the New Testament actually quotes of the Old is only a small sampling of that "fulfilling" of Moses, of the prophets, and of the Psalms to which Jesus pointed the disciples after His Resurrection.[18]

In what follows we gather for Lutheran education some of the resources available for probing the Scriptures in terms of their "theological reality" as the Word of God (the vertical line).

In teaching us the Scriptures our Lord must often bring us down first into depression, guilt, and utter hopelessness. Until we are brought low in this way we, like His disciples, seem unable to hear Him. We think we know but we do not know. Who can comprehend Psalm 51 if he has not himself entered into the shocking horror of David's self-discovery, how the hidden power of sin has secretly seduced, overwhelmed, and destroyed him? Who can grasp Psalm 42 if he has not himself experienced the devastating taunt, "Where is your God?" The Lord thrusts us into trial (Luther called it *tentatio*), so that His Word can break through and come alive with meaning for us. The Lutheran Confessors realized that no one can learn the doctrine of justification by faith through mere words. Only when a weak and terrified conscience has experienced rest and peace by the promises of God's grace in Christ, only then does the wonder of the Gospel shine for him in all its glory.[19] By their own experience of comfort the saints are equipped in turn to comfort one another with the Word of God which comforted them.[20] Thus the Gospel is proclaimed, as Luther put it, "through the mutual conversation and consolation of brethren." [21]

In its use of the Scriptures, Lutheran education will draw on the rich insight of the Confessions regarding the distinction between the Law and the Gospel.[22] God's Law speaks to us not only in the words of Scripture, but equally through experiences that expose to us the depths of our sinnerhood. Whatever happens to confront us with our guilt or futility is the voice of God's Law. If a conflict or disaster brings us down from a mountain of arrogance and plunges us into helplessness and despair, that too is God's Law. If we find ourselves compelled to demonstrate that we are worth something through the consuming intensity of our dedicated effort, that is the driving force of God's Law. If we find ourselves accused and confronted with realities of shame and weakness we dare not face, and if we are then compelled to hide our nakedness under tenuous "fig leaves," that is God's Law. If we are reminded that we came from the dirt, return to the dirt, and are nothing but dirt in between, that too is God's Law.

Once we realize how God's Law speaks in the very experience of our own living, we become the more able to hear that same Law speak in the Scriptures. By the mutual interplay of Biblical wisdom and of life, we grow to understand both the Scriptures and the nature of human lostness. Yet it is against this very Law that the Gospel breaks through in a flash of glory and love from the darkness of the cross, unexpected, beyond imagination. By the Law and the Gospel, we are given to know the truth about ourselves as sinners, and the glory and honor to which God raises us by free grace in the knowledge of Christ and the Father. To see *that* in Scripture, and to watch for it in all study of Scripture, is to use the Scriptures rightly as the Word of God.

Lutheran education's grasp of the Scriptures as God's Word will be enriched also as it discovers everywhere the three intimately related aspects of the Gospel we unfolded earlier. In text after text the Scriptures confer on us the *sonship* which was the glory of Israel and which is now ours in Christ. By way of that sonship the Scriptures promise us an eternal *inheritance* also, and assure us that our Father in heaven will meanwhile pour out His good gifts day by day and deliver us from evil. As children and heirs of God, the Scriptures call us to *serve* God and conform our life to His commandments in love for one another. His commandments are not distant and hard, but nearby, easy and light.[23] When our will is to do His will, that is when we know both Christ and the Father, as well as the authority of God's Word.[24] Thus the divine music of the Word of God fills the Scriptures, eager to be heard by any whose hearts are ready to listen.

Lutheran education will know the secret also of *discovering Christ* in all the Scriptures. Jesus died in total loneliness. Not only Israel but even His disciples had allied themselves in sinnerhood with the Gentiles, leaving Him to tread the winepress alone.[25] At that eternal moment all that God had ever said about sonship, life, and inheritance converged on Jesus only. He alone fulfilled the law. He alone loved the Father with all His heart, and His neighbor as Himself. He alone received the kingdom promised to Israel—not for His own sake only, but for ours. Therefore whenever the Scriptures of Moses, the prophets, and the Psalms speak of the people of God, they are speaking ultimately only of Christ! If these Scriptures now speak to us and about us, they do so only by the grace God has conferred on us through our baptism into Jesus' name. To read the Scriptures with that vision is to hear God talking to Christ and about Christ in every-' thing He says to His people. Through Christ we know the Scriptures, in order that by the Scriptures we may know Christ. Thus we begin to grasp the depths of John's marvellous summation, "The Word was made flesh" (John 1:14).

In searching the Scriptures, Lutheran education will want to examine with special care the substantive content enclosed in quotation marks, when God Himself has been introduced as the speaker. For example, Paul reports that *God said* to him, "My grace is sufficient for you, for my power is made perfect in weakness" (2 Cor. 12:9). Here we have a vivid example of how the Word of God from heaven comes down to intersect Paul's historical experience. What Paul tells us of his thorn in the flesh and his wrestling with God in prayer belongs to the "historical reality" of Scripture. But now the vertical "theological reality" breaks in, straight out of the cross of Christ. God's Word destroys the natural wisdom by which Paul thought he "knew" what was "good" for him and what was "evil." The sparks of the Spirit fly. The Word hits home and has its powerful effect. Now Paul understands his own *true power,* perfected in his very weakness! He can trust the Father to manifest His grace in the strangest ways, through "insults, hardships, persecutions, calamities." As we in our own historical humanity identify with Paul's pain and wrestling, the Word which Paul heard intersects our own hearts also. The Scriptures open wide to our understanding. We comprehend their wonder as the Word of God!

Lutheran education will also take special note of texts which preserve for us the response of saints who heard such a "Word" from God, even though the direct Word they heard is not recorded. From their response we can readily capture again what God said to evoke that particular testimony. For example, David could hardly sing, "The Lord is my Shepherd" (Psalm 23), if the Lord had not first said to him, "I will be your Shepherd" with all that such a promise implies. Or again, when we think of the Lord's Prayer and its petitions, it is enriching to ask *what God has said* to Jesus and through Him to us, which now makes that kind of praying possible. For it is God Himself who initiates any conversation we have with Him. Our response reflects what God has first said to us. Therefore if we already know a pattern of what God's Word is about, we are able to capture that Word in its rich beauty out of the very prayers and praises of the saints in the Scriptures.

Lutheran education will treasure Scripture as a gold mine. It will also yearn to mine that gold more effectively. Often the gold is not as ready to be grasped as may first appear. For example, in Luke 10:38-42 Mary sits at Jesus' feet to hear "his Word," while Martha concentrates on getting dinner. When things get out of hand, Martha reproves Jesus for "not caring." The rescue she desires in her "anxious and troubled" moment is simple. Jesus should tell her sister to help her and not leave her to serve alone. Jesus knows, however, that the passing help Mary gives will by no means free Martha from the root cause of her anxiety. What Martha really needs is a more enduring rest, which cannot "be taken away from her." Martha needs "the good portion" which "Mary has chosen." If we now are to mine the text in order to know what the "Word" *said* which meant so much to Mary, let our own human anxieties first help us understand the pressures which so overwhelmed Martha. Why could not Martha be relaxed and good humored about her limitations and frustrations? Why was it so important for her to succeed in being the perfect hostess? Whom was Martha really serving with all her sweat and effort? What image was she trying to salvage when she stormed in to accuse both her sister and her Guest of "not caring"? What "Word" did Jesus want to share with Martha which could set her free from her need to project an image of gracious hostessing on the one hand, and from the terrifying collapse of her own adequacies on the other? Other texts may help us here, for example, Luke 12:22-34. The point is that we do not fully know the story of Mary and Martha until we have mined from it that enduring Word of comfort which has power to turn a harried Martha into a relaxed Mary.

Sometimes the Word of God is buried so deeply beneath the surface of the Scriptures that it is hardly worth the effort to mine it. The possibility of discovering riches in unexpected places must never be foreclosed, of course. Yet for the church's ordinary use of the Scriptures the genealogies of 1 Chron. 1-9 would seem to be simply technical material. The sense of identity they inculcate in terms of our continuing participation in humanity, in Abraham, and in the God of Israel, can be mined far more simply in many other places.

Finally, Lutheran education will be on the alert for false stumbling blocks so that it may "teach the way of God truthfully" (Matt. 22: 16). It will not invoke a supposed authority of Scripture on matters of superstitious curiosity or of merely intellectual information which distract hearts from the true "way of God." Scripture is abused when its words are made to predict coming events through exotic but superficial applications of its apocalyptic imagery (as in Ezekiel, Daniel, Zechariah, and Revelation). Scripture is equally abused when the Bible is summoned to be the authoritative source of historical, geographical, and other "scientific" information. In both cases the authority of the Scriptures is misunderstood, and the real meaning of the Scriptures as "the Word of God" is altogether diluted and confused. If Lutheran education is to "teach the way of God truthfully," it needs to recognize such alien voices for what they are. Only so can it be the faithful instrument of the Word of God.

Let us define that "Word" once again. The Word of God has to do with the Law that exposes and judges us in our sin, and the Gospel of the cross which sets us free. It has to do with the honoring of Christ and the comforting of our terrified hearts through His name. It has to do with the wonder of our forgiveness and sonship, our unfailing hope and inheritance, and our joyful servanthood and free obedience in the family of God. This is the Spirit's Word. When our hearts grasp this Word by faith, then we live under the smile of a gracious God who holds us in His everlasting love. Then he can form us in His own image, so that we in turn may extend His love to one another and to our world. This Word of God is the uniqueness and glory, the truth and authority, the light and clarity of the Scriptures. Nothing else.

SCRIPTURE AS THE LANGUAGE OF MEN (HISTORICAL REALITY)

It is vital for Lutheran education to distinguish between the historical reality of Scripture (horizontal line) and the theological (vertical line). Given that distinction, together with an enriched joy and confidence in the sustaining Word of God from heaven which permeates all of Scripture, Lutheran education will not be ashamed of the Bible's full participation in human literature and history. It will not compromise the authentic historicity of the Scriptures by invoking an erroneous understanding of the Bible's inspiration and authority. On the contrary, Lutheran education will recognize that the revolution in Biblical studies is a gift from God to be accepted without fear and used to His glory. Our Lord has not only given us the Scriptures, He is determined also to open their message to us in its full riches. To that end He must first destroy the dross by which we had bound His Word in a false halo.

We cannot explore the findings of that revolution at this time. Certain areas in which contemporary Biblical studies have seemed to pose so great a threat are well known in our Synod. They have to do with the authorship of Biblical books, with the formation of the Pentateuch in the Old Testament and of the Gospels in the New, with the use the New Testament makes of Old Testament texts, with the understanding of literary forms, with the historicity and facticity of persons and events, with the authenticity of Jesus' own utterances in relation to the voices of witnesses who breathed His Spirit and spoke in His name,[26] and with the interchangeable identification between Jesus and His church.[27]

Through the purifying, Lutheran education will understand that all such questions have to do with the "historical reality" of Scripture. In terms of our diagram they belong to the horizontal line and not to the vertical. It is not appropriate, therefore, to approach such questions by appealing to the Bible's inspiration and authority. We must rather summon the soundest reasoning of which we are capable, based on a careful gathering and examination of the literary evidence. For the Bible belongs to the world, to our own humanity. Its "historical reality" in no way undermines or compromises the truth that Scripture is "the Word of God." On the contrary, the historical reality of Scripture is precisely what makes all "exegesis" possible, that is, all the hard work that goes into understanding it. And this historical reality, properly harnessed and valued, becomes the very arena and occasion for the vertical "Word of God" to intersect our own actual humanness and experience.

The task of Lutheran education in relation to the Bible's historical reality will not be simply to teach the so-called "assured results" of modern Biblical scholarship. Far more, the task is to give students the opportunity to examine the evidences and to follow the reasonings in order to develop an awareness of how such findings occur and how they become persuasive. In this way we properly honor and challenge the God-given minds of our learners. We set them free under God to think for themselves, to test everything, and to embrace what seems convincing. We teach them also to hold in abeyance, modify, or even reject whatever does not seem persuasive. Above all, however, the task is to expect, seek and discover how a clearer understanding of any text in its literary and historical dimension (horizontal line) may open the way for the Bible's "theological reality" (vertical line) to intersect us and to pierce our hearts with a deeper understanding.

Thereby Lutheran education will stir up and call into use whatever gifts the Spirit has planted in any of Christ's saints. Surely the Lord intends to raise up in His Church some who are both inclined and equipped to participate intensively in the continuing exploration of the Bible on the historical level. These individuals will then do their work, not in the pride of their reason, but in the humility and confidence of saints who fear, love, and trust their Lord. They will delight in His Holy Scriptures. They will want nothing more than to serve Christ and His people with whatever gifts they have.

To that end it is necessary for Lutheran education to know what is meant by "historical-critical" study of the Bible. Only so can it also repudiate the false accusations which our dross has continually raised against it.

To call the Bible "historical" is to recognize that it belongs to human history and literature. Humanly intelligible events and situations occasioned its writing at every point. The authors of Scripture were as human as we are. They drew on their total insight and experience, including their whole relationship to and knowledge of God, so as to express the thoughts of their minds in words and sentences which they expected their human readers to understand. "Exegesis" (our struggle to understand the author and his writings more fully) is possible because, by God's own creative wisdom, our mental processes correspond to those of these holy writers. Exegesis enables us to play back with increasing refinement and depth the very insight and meaning which passed through the mind of a Biblical writer, as he put down the words and sentences that the Spirit moved him to record for our learning. The words anyone speaks or writes, if they are at all serious, are simply the vehicle by which ideas are transmitted. By such words the hearer or reader has opportunity to share in the perceptions and conceptions of the author. The process of communication implies an interaction between speaker and hearer. Exegesis is the tool that sharpens our capacity to hear.

Because the Bible derives from, belongs to, and expresses the history and experience of men, it is subject to every process of rational inquiry which may contribute toward understanding more clearly what it says. That the Bible is to be interpreted historically is not merely a matter of right and freedom but of necessity and divine command. After all, we did not create our minds. God did. It is He who made both the writers and the readers of the Bible to be thinking men. To use our minds fully belongs to our serving and obeying God. A piety which invokes "child-like faith" as an excuse for *not* thinking, or imagines that it serves God by "sacrificing the intellect," is not trusting and serving God at all! It is simply burying a God-given talent in the ground.[28]

The Christian exegete who does his hard mental work in faith is not afraid that his findings will destroy Scripture as the Word of God. On the contrary, disciplined thinking is the very instrument by which he searches that Word, joyfully confident that as he grasps more fully the "historical reality" at any point, the "theological reality" will break through with sparks of Spirit, truth, and power beyond all expectations.

"Historical thinking," so understood, is inevitably also "critical." To the *mind of dross* the term "critical" suggests the blasphemy of an arrogant reason which dares to "criticize" and "find fault" with the Word of God. That is *not* what the term "critical" means. Critical thinking does not criticize the Scripture at all. On the contrary, it is critical only of *our own* fallible impressions of the Bible. Critical thinking puts what we thought we knew to the test. It exposes where our thinking was mistaken. It seeks a clearer and truly persuasive understanding of each specific historical reality.

To understand all this we need to become more consciously aware of how the human mind works. Lutheran education above all will be alert to distinguish "critical thinking" from the "noncritical." Our ordinary thinking and knowing is mostly noncritical. We see a chair, know immediately what it is, and sit down in it. We do not expect to be deceived, nor do we pause for the least moment to wonder whether we may be misinterpreting what our eyes have so clearly told us. "Seeing is believing." From perception to knowledge, that is the simple sequence of our ordinary experience. Our minds are indeed involved in the process. Memory and association have come into play. But we are not consciously aware that any "thinking" occurred. Why should we think about, or question, what we so obviously know?

"Critical thinking" occurs when we are suddenly caught short and forced to look again. We suspect that our first impression was in error. Something does not look right. We examine the evidence more closely. Our mind is careful now. It rejects, rethinks, tests, and arrives at a fuller and more persuasive understanding. That "chair" is in reality a bedside commode. To sit on it unknowingly might be a bit embarrassing. We are conscious now that we are thinking, aware that our first impression was inadequate and mistaken. We are not "criticizing" the commode, however. What we are criticizing is simply our own perception. The fallibility did not lie in the "chair" but in our "thinking" it was a chair!

Critical thinking is revelatory. It is sometimes a source of good humor. Often, however, it is not a bit funny. We thought we understood what a brother was saying, but events proved us wrong. In the meantime our wrong thinking yielded grave injustice and slander against him. Noncritical thinking frequently gives birth to tragedy. A man thinks he hears a burglar and shoots his own son.

The "scientific revolution" of the post-Reformation centuries was largely a systematic and conscious application of "critical" thinking to test things people had long taken for granted. People thought they saw a hard dome of sky (firmament) overhead holding up the stars. They thought that manure gives spontaneous birth to maggots, earth to snakes and grasses, and ponds to fish. But such "noncritical" inferences did not stand up to closer examination of the evidence. It was a shattering age. For a long time people wondered whether it was possible to know anything with certainty. In terms of new knowledge, however, the scientific revolution was fantastically productive.

"Historical-critical" means that "critical thinking" is applied consciously and systematically to the study of history. History, of course, has to do not with natural phenomena, but with people and human society. For this reason the historian faces complications far beyond those of the natural scientist. The natural scientist knows that his own mind is fallible; therefore he wants to test his theoretical understanding of reality in every way possible. But the historian is dealing with the thought processes and fallibility of more minds than merely his own. The people he is trying to know in past history were thinking people. As thinking people they reacted in terms of the way they understood themselves and things around them. As thinking people they recorded their impressions and interpretations of what they had witnessed, experienced, and researched. At every level the historian gathers into his own thinking, by way of words and evidence which history has left behind, what other people were once thinking. Thereby he comes to understand better why they thought the way they thought, said things the way they said them, and acted the way they acted. The historian must "reconstruct" it all into a single coherent picture which makes simple and persuasive sense. In doing that kind of work, the historian's own humanness and his understanding of how his own mind functions are a great and basic asset.

Lutheran education must be concerned to develop an enlightened understanding of what the human mind entails and how it operates. Teachers and students together need to be aware of the mind's limitations. They need to know not only *that* our minds are fallible, but also *how* mistaken judgments occur, and *why* any human level of inquiry must fall short of complete, absolute, and final "truth." Such awareness is essential equipment for anyone who is gifted and inclined to do "critical" thinking in any area of human thought.

A Christian exegete who brings critical thinking to bear in Bible study will realize that he is dealing with two different orders of "truth." In approaching the Bible's "historical reality" (horizontal line), he is seeking what makes sense by sound reason. If at some point all the evidence falls into place so that now something makes sense which did not make sense before, he will accept this new understanding as true, real, and workable. Such "believing" is not of the heart and Holy Spirit, of course, but of the thinking mind. It is a matter of persuasion on the basis of evidence. It is also not absolute. Some day the exegete may change his mind, at least in part, as more evidence enters the picture and requires a revision of his thinking.

That is why Biblical scholars frequently disagree in their interpretations. What makes such good and persuasive sense to one does not fully convince another. The searching and the exchange of insights must simply continue. No external authority such as majority vote can impose as "truth" what remains unpersuasive to even a minority of one! After all, one man is always the first to see what no one else has yet noticed!

The goal of the interpreter in his search for "truth" on the historical plane is simply to understand texts in such a way that all questions are answered. The exegete is *not* making the text say "whatever he pleases," as the dross has frequently charged. If any interpreter should be misled by his own preconceptions, other exegetes will quickly expose the fallacy he himself did not notice. Neither are exegetes concerned that truth of the sort they are seeking is never final. They do know that when a breakthrough occurs which makes convincing sense, which answers many nagging questions, and which clears up a whole range of confusions and blind alleys, such an insight exerts great power. It cannot be ignored and evaded by any serious student. It "answers" a real problem! Though it is always subject to further challenge, re-examination, and refinement, it must be taken into account as a building block toward inquiry into other areas.

In all of this we are dealing with truth on the level of man in his world, as the human mind seeks and understands truth. The Christian exegete, however, is looking ultimately for something more. He seeks the truth of the Spirit of God which does not stop at the mind of man, but penetrates the *heart*. The heart of the sinner is not comforted by exegetical insights, after all, but by the Word of divine grace from the cross of Christ. Paul calls this "the truth of the Gospel" (Gal. 2:5, 14). It comes by words, of course, and by the sacraments, but what the Word conveys is the grace of God in the Christ who is "the Way, the Truth, and the Life" (John 14:6). This truth is the Rock that never fails, our sure foundation against which even the gates of hell cannot prevail.[29] Exegetes may be right or wrong. Their rightness or wrongness neither saves nor condemns them. The Christian exegete sets no hope in his rightness as an interpreter, but only in the righteousness of faith in his Lord, Jesus Christ.

Thus the Christian exegete is two things simultaneously. In terms of the Bible's "theological reality" he is a hungry child of God, eager to hear the Word of God and feed on it as his Bread of Life. In terms of the "historical reality" of Scripture, he is a disciplined historian, facing all the hardships and hazards of the historical enterprise, but not afraid to use his mind. For his work is a divine calling. It is not his business to worry about consequences. He simply entrusts these to the Lord as he also thanks the Lord for the fruits of his work.

But if historical study still seems to threaten the Bible, such fears derive not from the gold but from the dross that still afflicts us. Our living Lord calls us simply to trust His Book to Him. He gave it. He can well take care of it! "The Scripture cannot be broken," He has promised (John 10:35). If ever it *seems* to us that the Scriptures are being broken, what is really being shattered is not the Scriptures at all, but only our own long-treasured but mistaken opinions and confidences. Nothing will really be lost. The Lord who holds the Scriptures will hold us also.

Footnotes for Chapter IV

[1] The quotation derives not directly from Synod's current controversy, but from its background in seventeenth century Lutheranism as summarized in Robert D. Preus, *The Theology of Post-Reformation Lutheranism* (St. Lous: Concordia Publishing House, 1970), p. 298. It is helpful to be aware that the dross with which we are currently wrestling is no distinctively Missouri Synod fallacy, but came into our heritage from much earlier sources. It may be useful to amplify the quotation a bit further:

"Any and every attempt to reduce or condition the authority of Scripture constitutes the open resistance against God and defiance of His lordship of which all men are so terribly prone. . . . The only possible response to God speaking is faith. And this response always involves casting down reasonings and every high thing that exalts itself against the knowledge of God; it always involves the painfully humiliating, mortifying *sacrificium intellectus* [sacrifice of the intellect], so repugnant to all men. To bow to the authority of Scripture often means believing in what the natural reason of man considers impossible and absurd. . . . Therefore it is absolutely necessary for us to take our mind and thoughts captive to the Scriptures."

[2] Thus Resolution 3–09 of the Missouri Synod's New Orleans Convention (July 6-13, 1973) includes the "*Resolved,* that the Synod repudiate that attitude toward Holy Scripture, particularly as regards its authority and clarity, which reduces to theological opinion or exegetical questions, matters which are in fact clearly taught in Scripture (e.g., facticity of miracle accounts and their details; historicity of Adam and Eve as real persons; the fall of Adam and Eve into sin as a real event, to which original sin and its imputation upon all succeeding generations of mankind must be traced; the historicity of every detail in the life of Jesus as recorded by the evangelists; predictive prophecies in the Old Testament which are in fact Messianic; the doctrine of angels; the Jonah account, etc.)." *Convention Proceedings*, p. 139.

³ Ephesians 4:1-6.

⁴ From "A Comparative Study of Varying Contemporary Approaches to Biblical Interpretation," A Report of the Commission on Theology and Church Relations, The Lutheran Church—Missouri Synod, March, 1973. Issued as a tract, but published also in the New Orleans *Convention Workbook* (1973), pp. 435-448. For the citations we quote, see p. 447. These same quotations recur in a subsequent CTCR document, "Report on Dissent," September 1974, p. 19.

⁵ Hymns 473 and 370 in *The Lutheran Hymnal* (St. Louis: Concordia Publishing House, 1941). Our hymnody at times reflects also the ambiguity of "two foundations," however. For example, in Hymn 373 we sing, "By grace I'm saved, grace free and boundless; My soul, believe and doubt it not. Why stagger at this word of promise? *Hath Scripture ever falsehood taught? Nay; then this word must true remain:* By grace thou, too, shalt heav'n obtain." The power of our believing seems not to derive, then, from the Spirit in the very Word which conveys the promise. We believe the promise rather because we *already believe a prior word,* namely, the inerrancy and inspiration of the Scriptures.

⁶ Resolution 3-09, *Convention Proceedings* (1973), pp. 136-137.

⁷ Something like this seems to be implied when it is argued, "The question cannot be whether the Gospel did not come first, before the written Word; but rather, whether *we today* have any other rule, judge, norm, touchstone, by which the Gospel may be *known among us* than Holy Scripture." *Ibid.,* p. 136. Emphasis ours.

⁸ The Missouri Synod has tried to prevent the Scriptures from becoming a foundation separate from the Gospel of Christ, by invoking a distinction between the "material" and the "formal" principles in Lutheran theology. According to this distinction, Lutheranism's "material principle" is the Gospel, and its "formal principle" the Holy Scriptures. See, for example, "A Statement of Scriptural and Confessional Principles" (SSCP) IV,C; "Gospel and Scripture: The Interrelationship of the Material and Formal Principles in Lutheran Theology," A Report of the Commission on Theology and Church Relations, The Lutheran Church—Missouri Synod, November, 1972; also Resolution 3-09, *Convention Proceedings* (1973), p. 136.

But this distinction, too, is a logical fallacy. In their authentic integrality, "material principle" would refer to the content of an idea, and "formal" to the form of words in which that idea is then expressed. We imply both the distinction and the integrality when we say, for example, "I know *what* I want to say (material), but I don't know *how* to say it (formal)."

As long as "the Word of God" means *the Gospel,* the integrality between material and formal principles is very clear. The "material" of the Gospel is the grace of God in Christ toward sinners, as SSCP IV,C also acknowledges. The "form" of that Gospel is the very words in which this grace of God in Christ is expressed and proclaimed. That is what Lutheran theology has in mind when it calls the Gospel the "means of grace" and the "external word," as in Augsburg Confession V. Paul implies as much in 1 Cor. 2:11-13, where the Spirit is described as knowing the "thoughts of God" (material principle) and then putting those thoughts into "words" for our sakes (formal principle).

When the Missouri Synod calls *Scripture* the "formal principle," however, this integrality of thought and word is violated and broken. We are distracted now from thinking of the Gospel itself as *words*. We are prone to attribute the power of the Spirit not to the words that proclaim Christ, but to the divinely authored Bible, as SSCP explicitly does in IV,D! At the same time we forget that our "material principle" is simply "the Gospel of the gracious justification of the sinner through faith in Jesus Christ" (SSCP IV,C). We now begin to supplement the "material" which Christians must accept, with all kinds of "other matters taught in the Scriptures which are not a part of the 'Gospel' " (SSCP IV,C,4).

Only as our dross is exposed and our gold refined can we grasp the full dimensions of that logical and theological confusion.

[9] Matt. 22:42; John 3:18.

[10] Num. 14:10; John 8:59; 10:31; Acts 7:58, 14:5,19.

[11] That "Word" and "Gospel" are interchangeable terms is directly apparent, for example, in Acts 15:10; Rom. 10:8, 15-18; Eph. 1:13; Col. 1:5; 1 Thess. 1:4; 2:13.

[12] The symbol of the vertical line, marked by the cross, intersecting our own name, and piercing our heart, is borrowed from Dona Hoffman, *Yes Lord* (St. Louis: Concordia Publishing House, 1975).

[13] Heb. 4:12.

[14] Jer. 23:29.

[15] Ps. 33:15.

[16] John 15:26; Luke 24:28; Acts 1:8; 5:32; 10:39-41; 1 Pet. 5:1; 1 John 1:1-3.

[17] Luke 11:8-13.

[18] Luke 24:25–27, 32,44-46.

[19] AC XX,15-17.

[20] 2 Cor. 1:3-7.

[21] Smalcald Articles III,iv.

[22] "All Scripture should be divided into these two chief doctrines, the law and the promises" (Apology IV,5). "The distinction between law and Gospel is an especially brilliant light which serves the purpose that the Word of God may be rightly divided and the writings of the holy prophets may be explained and understood correctly" (Formula of Concord V,1).

[23] Deut. 30:11-14; Matt. 11:29-30.

[24] John 7:17.

[25] Is. 63:3; Rev. 19:13-16.

[26] Luke 10:16.

[27] Acts 9:4.

[28] Matt. 25:18,25.

[29] Matt. 7:24; 16:18.

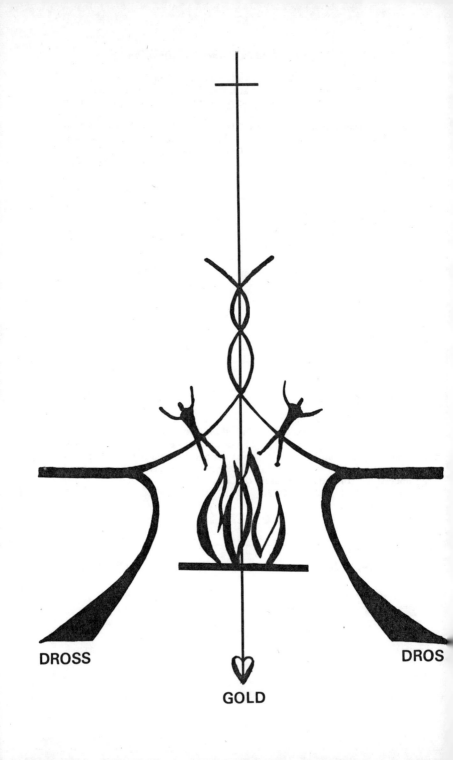

DROSS

DROS

GOLD

Epilogue

Some twenty-five years ago the Board of Parish Education of the Lutheran Church—Missouri Synod had in hand what seemed a simple but very necessary project. It undertook to formulate for the church a clear and unified "philosophy'" of Lutheran education. A decade of effort involving the gifts of many able and dedicated people ended in futility, however, and the project had to be abandoned.

Looking back through the fire, it is not hard to see why it had to fail. Any "philosophy" of Lutheran education would have to be based squarely on "the Word of God." Yet in the Missouri Synod that very term embodied a critical but unnoticed ambiguity. In one sense, it meant the proclaimed Gospel of salvation by faith in Christ, pointing to Christ alone as our one foundation and cornerstone. In another sense, "the Word of God" meant the Holy Scriptures as the sure foundation upon which the Synod wanted to erect its theological edifice. These two thrusts might have been unified and compatible if Synod had understood the authority of Scripture to derive from Christ and the Word and Spirit which proclaimed Him. Such was not the case, however. In the mind of Synod the authority of Scripture was a function not of its Gospel, but of its verbal and plenary inspiration.

Thus the dross we defined in the preceding chapters was unwittingly mixed and equated with the gold of the Gospel. Its effect was to set Lutheran education on two foundations, each leading to its own set of consequences. There was no way a single and coherent "philosophy" could do equal justice to both.

THE END OF THE FIRE

The drawing which heads this chapter attempts to visualize this dichotomy and its consequences. Its central feature is the Word of God. We depict the Word again as a razor sharp vertical line descending from God to us and bringing Christ and the cross to our hearts. This Word is our gold. It has always been our gold. The entanglement of impurities could not keep it from being gold, neither does the Lord's fire harm it. This golden Word alone sustains us through the fire. It is our everlasting Rock and the glory of the Scriptures. By this Word we dare to praise God even through our great distress. We know now that His fire was sent not to destroy us but only to expose and rid us of our dross.

The drawing depicts next a twining which entered to confuse and entangle us. The twining identified itself as "the Word of God." We thought it was gold and did not distinguish it from our golden Gospel. For a long period, therefore, our church was caught in an unrecognized ambiguity. We used the term "the Word of God" to mean the Gospel, but also to mean the inspired Scriptures. In our theology we designated the Gospel as the "material principle" and the Scriptures as the "formal principle," and thought that these terms defined and assured the integrality of the two.[1]

An uneasy tension persisted, however, and was never really resolved. In retrospect it shows itself in the way various pastors approached confirmation instruction. The Missouri Synod's familiar "Short Explanation" of Luther's Small Catechism began by defining the Bible as "the Word of God" in terms of its inspiration.[2] Some pastors, after spending a session or two on this introductory material, would hardly ever refer to it again. For others this section deserved continuing attention in view of the anti-Biblical rationalism they saw invading the church. Still others passed it by entirely, preferring to plunge immediately into the substantive message of the Scriptures— by way of the Commandments, the Creed, or Baptism. These alternative approaches already implied differing "philosophies" of Lutheran education, but no one noticed any such significance.

The fire in our drawing derived its first heat from conflicts which many teachers and pastors saw arising between the Bible and science.[3] The heat intensified, however, as more and more pastors encountered "the historical-critical method" of Bible study and were forced to reckon with it. As the fire spread, anxieties increased. Pastors, teachers, and lay people were compelled to react in some way.

One such reaction we might call "liberalism." It consisted in a loosening grip on the very concept of the Word of God and of the Holy Scriptures as our "only rule and norm". One factor in such loosening, we suspect, was a valid concern that the church and the Word be relevant to what people really are in the contemporary world. Another factor may well have been the sense of a vacuum of personal meaning in "the Word of God" as we had taught it. The very ambiguity with which our Synod has been wrestling contributed, we think, toward creating that kind of vacuum. Authentic liberalism, however, does not seem to have been a major factor in causing the fire in our church.

The critical point of our conflict derives rather from the two sides of the ambiguity itself. The heat of the fire forced every pastor and teacher to accent and come to the defense of that meaning of "the Word of God" which had assumed primacy in his own understanding of Christian doctrine. The ambiguity which caused the ensuing division was not detected, however. Everybody still agreed that the "true treasure" of Lutheranism was *both* the holy inspired Scriptures *and* "the most holy Gospel of the glory and grace of God." [4] No one thought of himself as having to "chose" between these two. Those whose primary concern in the heat of the fire was to defend the inspiration and authority of the Bible did so, they insisted, for the Gospel's sake. On the other hand, those whose primary concern was for the Word of God as the Gospel of Christ quickly affirmed also their continuing faith in the inspiration and authority of the Scriptures. It was a matter of "both . . . and," not of "either . . . or."

Nevertheless, conversation between the parties became increasingly difficult. Each side would affirm the other's position with a conciliatory "of course" or "me too" or "I have no problem with that." Then would come an inevitable "but" of anxious demurrer, bringing the other "primacy" into play. After that the conversation seemed to stall. Nothing remained to be said, except to repeat points already made, only more loudly. Outsiders were baffled. If everybody agreed with the other, why the argument?

But the heat increased. Each side defined "the issue" by that understanding of "the Word of God" which held primacy in his own thinking. Some felt the church faced a decisive choice: *either* the inspired Scriptures *or* critical study. Everybody rejected what kept looming as an alternative choice: *either* Scripture *or* Gospel. Nobody saw the true "either . . . or" hidden like dross under the ambiguity of the key term, "the Word of God." Meanwhile the frustration of meaningful dialogue yielded a growing sense of despair. Brethren accused each other of being simply stubborn or closed. It was always the other side that would "not listen."

Our concern in this writing is not with persons in the controversy, or with what appear to be its "political" dimensions. We seek rather to understand the forces beneath the struggle, which have impelled the parties in opposing directions. For "we are not contending against flesh and blood," that is, against one another, Paul would remind us. The real enemy is rather "the principalities" and "the powers" which have trapped us secretly and unrecognized (Eph. 6:12). Such forces capitalized on our ambiguity and kept us from seeing our dross. We were affirming things as equal which could not be affirmed equally. By saying "both . . . and" without clearly distinguishing what we meant, we were not walking "uprightly according to the truth of the Gospel" (Gal. 2:14 AV), as Paul puts it in describing Peter's inadvertent compromise. Like Peter we were rather twisting, tilting, trying forcibly to hang on to two things which simply did not fit together in the way our tradition insisted they must. Each party among us was quick to detect such tilting and lack of uprightness in the other.

Consider, for example, those whose tilt was toward the primacy of the Gospel as the Word of God. On the one hand they spoke much of the Gospel, often very beautifully. On the other hand they continued to reassure their anxious brethren of their unqualified acceptance of the Scriptures as the Word of God. "Nothing has changed," they seemed to say, as they repeated in familiar words their full acceptance of the plenary inspiration, authority, and inerrancy of the Scriptures. But their brethren were not reassured. They saw compromise and dishonesty. They knew very well that something had changed. Critical study of the Bible would be impossible without some change of attitude toward the authority of the Scriptures. The ready inference was that "liberalism" and "rationalism" were entering to destroy our church and its doctrine, as it had previously undermined the truth and vitality of the Christian faith in other churches. "What else could I think?" a brother would say. Thereafter every appeal to "the Gospel" had the appearance of mere evasiveness, and every renewed protestation of loyalty to the Scriptures and to Article II of the Synod's constitution seemed only to confirm the deceitfulness of those who uttered it.

The impression of insincerity in those who took their stand on "the Gospel" added much to the heat of the fire. After all, if someone is prone to lie, it does not seem very useful to keep listening to him. In everything he says he is only trying to justify what cannot be justified and to give a show of right to what is not right. Thus conversation was impeded all the more. Everybody still agreed that the issue was theological. Nevertheless, in practice much polemic and action in the church was now conditioned by the personal distrust in which members of the Synod were holding their fellow members.

If we are now to "put the best construction on everything," we must seek some explanation other than deliberate deceitfulness for what came through as dishonesty. In retrospect it appears that our dross, our hidden ambiguity, had simply trapped us. Consider how various people reacted when critical study of the Scriptures began to invade our church. Those who took "the Word of God" to mean primarily the inspired Bible could not help but regard such study as "rationalism," that is, the imposition of man's reason over God's Word. On the other hand, those who thought of "the Word of God" primarily as the Gospel did not see Scripture as necessarily threatened by what was happening in critical study. In their minds critical study was not an enemy to be repelled, but a challenge the church dared not evade. They discovered that it was no easy matter to meet that challenge. Many a brother can tell of the torment he experienced personally as he tried to deal honestly on the one hand with his own and Synod's traditional understanding of the Bible's inspiration, and on the other hand with inescapable questions critical study was raising. All this belonged to the Lord's fire. Its effect was to generate a revised, but as yet undefined, conception of what the Scriptures really are as the inspired and inerrant "Word of God."

The dilemma in which such brethren were now caught was not readily apparent even to them. They were understanding the inspiration, authority, and inerrancy of the Scriptures in terms of the Gospel. They found this understanding of the Word to be both Scriptural and Confessional. By it they affirmed their loyalty to Article II of the Synod's constitution "without reservation." Scripture is indeed "the written Word of God and the only rule and norm of faith and of practice."

The trap was that the *meaning* of this confession differed now from the meaning they themselves had once found in these very same words. Their brothers knew only the older meaning, equated this with "pure doctrine," and defended it as "Synod's doctrinal position." But what was really Synod's "doctrinal position"? Much of our tradition supported the view that Scripture is "the Word of God" by virtue of God's authorship of every word. Nevertheless our Synod also took its stand on the Lutheran Confessions; and in the Confessions, as many among us were increasingly convinced, the authority of the Scriptures as "the Word of God" coincides with the authority of the Gospel. If brethren were reaching the latter persuasion, were they really "changing our Synod's doctrine," as was so often charged? Who would judge such a question, and what would be the standard for judging it?

Questions such as these constituted a vast hidden agenda. The ambiguity, however, prevailed unnoticed and undefined. Therefore those who had in reality been changed by their wrestlings with critical study could still insist that they were not deviating from Synod's doctrinal and confessional position. They did not realize, apparently, how deceptive and incomprehensible that insistence would appear to those in the church who most needed to be reassured. Still less did they realize that the change in their understanding was truly revolutionary, not only for themselves, but for the whole church. The very foundations of the Christian faith were at stake. They were learning what it means to stand on the Word of divine promise in *the Gospel* as the one, sure, and unshakeable foundation even of the Bible! Yet in the eyes of brothers who regarded *the inspired Bible* as the foundation of all faith and theology, this "Gospel" without the undergirding of the Bible would seem to be pure human speculation, detached from history, drawn out of "thin air," and *no foundation at all!*

So successful was the disguise of the dross that even those who had begun to identify the authority of the Scriptures with that of the Gospel continued to pay tribute to the dross. They used old words like "inspired" and "inerrant" without rejecting or even challenging their mistaken application. They were quite willing for others to consider the Scriptures authoritative on the basis of their divine authorship, as though the alternative points of view were harmless and equally viable options, and a matter of "freedom" in the Gospel. Thereby they sealed the impression that they were "liberal," doctrinally indifferent, permissive, and unconcerned for the truth. Regardless of what explanations we may now offer, the net effect was one of compromise and insincerity, of not walking uprightly according to the truth of the Gospel.

Epilogue

But there was a tilting and dissembling also on the other side. It too was a product of the hidden dross, inadvertent and unintentional. Nevertheless it was real. Those who took their stand on the Gospel alone and yet failed to see their own tilting, readily detected a lack of uprightness in their brothers. It seemed that those who made Scripture their battle line in defending the Gospel were trying to live simultaneously in two different worlds. On the one hand they professed the Gospel as the heart and center of Christian faith and theology. In practice, however, they deliberately removed the Gospel from that center and declared it to be "not the issue" in the controversy. They professed to accept without reservation the Scriptures as "the only rule and norm of faith and of practice" (Article II), yet in controversy they based their appeal not on clear Biblical texts but on "Synod's doctrinal position." They professed to believe with Article VIII,C of Synod's constitution that "all matters of doctrine and of conscience shall be decided only by the Word of God" and all others "by majority vote," yet in controversy they were determined to settle doctrinal matters by voting at a convention. They professed to know what all Lutherans know, that erroneous human traditions can arise in any church, yet without so much as subjecting our Synod's tradition to testing they upheld Synod's doctrinal position by majority vote as pure and in accordance with "the Word of God." They professed to believe that "the sword of the Spirit is the Word of God" (Eph. 6:17), yet for their weapon in this battle they turned to the power of the synodical institution and to the Handbook, counting on the authority of elected officials to bring dissidents into line. They professed to believe in the holy Christian Church as the communion of saints, marked by Word and sacrament, and called to share in one another's gifts for the common good. In practice, however, the synodical headquarters acted like a "hierarchy." It asserted its dominion over districts and congregations. It treated called ministers of Christ as though they were merely "employees." It summoned brothers in Christ to account not for clearly specified doctrinal reasons or for patent sins, but for resisting its authority and being insubordinate.

Therefore the fire raged. Fueled by grave suspicions of deceit and lack of personal integrity, it set people against people. Efforts were made to cool the fire, to define the issues, to get conversations going, and to achieve reconciliation. Nothing seemed to work. No compromise solutions, however carefully negotiated, withstood the test of reality. Each side called upon the other to repent. Each summoned against the other what he thought was the Lord's clear Word of judgment. Each pressed his own case, sure of his rightness, and doing battle for the Lord. The monumental tragedy of schism loomed, and if not schism, then at least utter frustration and wounds unhealed. It was a time of dismay and helplessness, a time for crying to the Lord.

The Lord has heard our cry. He had to keep the fire going until our ambiguity was revealed and the dross exposed for all to see. Once that had happened we as His people would know our gold, let the dross go, and rest in Him alone. In that moment the church would discover itself to be truly pure, glorious, without spot or wrinkle, holy and without blemish before Him.[5] For our purifying does not depend upon our works individually or as a Synod. It does not depend upon the perfection of our exegetical insights or doctrinal formulations. Our purity lies solely in the forgiving grace of God, sealed to us in the cross of Christ through our baptism and His supper. We seek no other purity than that. When we have that purity, everything is pure. If we lack that purity nothing is pure.

Therefore we find peace and rest in the grace of our Lord Jesus Christ alone. Whatever our guilt has been, it is forgiven. Whatever accusations stand against us, His cross has erased them. If we have been wrong, Christ is our eternal rightness. If we have gone through great tribulation, so has He, and He is our victory. If we have been divided, He is our unity. If we have faced the terror of total helplessness, He is our hope and our power. By His grace we can look upon and cling to one another in love and forgiveness, in humility and mutual honor. Together we look to Christ, our one Lord. He is our praise.

The Lord must love us very much to have invested such extraordinary effort in us. Surely He has not gone to all that trouble for nothing! Therefore we lift our eyes to Christ who has long since destroyed our shame and death, and brought us again to life. We are not afraid of tomorrow's uncertainties, so long as we walk with Him. In Him we shall learn to walk "uprightly according to the truth of the Gospel," no longer tilting. In Him we shall walk together as one Body, ready to be enriched by the gifts He invests in His members, not fearful to offer Him and one another even our weaknesses and fears as a gift. For we expect our God to turn even our tensions into an opportunity for greater love and common growth in Him who is our Head.

Our warfare is ended, and our iniquity is pardoned. We have received from the Lord's hand double grace for all our sins.[6] It is as though our "forty years" of anxious wilderness are over. We are ready to follow, as our Lord unfolds to us what is next.

HALLOWING GOD'S NAME

Lutheran education, we suggested earlier, may be defined simply and beautifully by Luther's explanation of the First Petition in his Small Catechism. God's name is hallowed

> when the Word of God is taught clearly and purely and we, as children of God, lead holy lives in accordance with it. Help us to do this, dear Father in heaven! But whoever teaches and lives otherwise than as the Word of God teaches, profanes the name of God among us. From this preserve us, heavenly Father.

The concept of "profaning God's name," like that of the purifying fire, has roots in Ezekiel. The house of Israel had forced God to "pour out [His] wrath upon them" by their compromising idolatries. Therefore, God "scattered them among the nations." As all the nations saw the defeat and scattering of Israel, they could only infer that Israel's God Himself was weak and defeated, unable to save His people! Thus Israel, in its very defeat and scattering, was proclaiming to the nations a false testimony regarding the Lord their God. *"They profaned my holy name,"* the Lord declares (Ezek. 36:18-21). Then comes the turning point, the surprising Word of hope. The Lord cannot allow His name to be held in such disrepute. "I had concern for my holy name," He says, and commands Ezekiel to tell His people

> Thus says the Lord God: It is not for your sake, O house of Israel, that I am about to act, but for the sake of my holy name, which you have profaned among the nations to which you came. And will vindicate the holiness of my great name . . . ; and the nations will know that I am the Lord, says the Lord God, when through you I vindicate my holiness before their eyes. For I will take you from the nations, and gather you from all the countries, and bring you into your own land. I will sprinkle clean water upon you, and . . . from all your idols I will cleanse you. A new heart I will give you, and a new spirit I will put within you (Ezek. 36:22-26).

The passage climaxes with the powerful reminder,

> It is not for your sake that I will act, says the Lord God; let that be known to you. Be ashamed and confounded for your ways, O house of Israel (Ezek. 36:32).

Today we are that "house of Israel." We have profaned God's holy name. Despite all our claims to possess the "pure doctrine," we were in reality not teaching His Word "clearly and purely." In defense of impurities we thought to be gold, we turned our wrath and accusation against one another. Thus we forced the Lord to send forth the full fury of His wrath upon us all. By our dispute and division we have witnessed falsely to the whole land concerning our God. We have proclaimed to the world a God who divides what Christ has united—a God who is served when members of Christ's one Body utilize organizational weapons to wage "holy war" against one another. We took upon ourselves the anxious burden of saving our Bible, our pure doctrine, and our church from whatever we thought was the enemy. People looking in upon us did not see us under the cross and marked by God's Word of love and peace. Thus the name of God was profaned among us, not only by the confusion of our teaching but also by our living.

Therefore the God of all grace had to intervene in His own way to save us from the enemy we did not even recognize. By the fire of His wrath He set about to vindicate "the holiness of [His] great name." He purified us in His own amazing way. He made us see what we could not see. He gathered us into His bosom, sprinkled upon us the clean water of our baptismal forgiveness, and created within us a clean heart and a right spirit. We did not deserve such grace or even dare to expect it. When we look back at what we were and did, we can only "be ashamed and confounded." But the name of our God, "Father, Son, and Holy Spirit," is greater than our shame.

His name is *holy*. That means that our God is different from anything we human sinners would ever imagine or expect. He distributes gifts unequally, as He will. He brings down and He lifts up, as He will. He chooses the ripeness of His time, as He will. The consummate surprise of His holy name is Calvary. There He confronted the totality of human guilt and shame not with wrath but with love, not in strength but in weakness, not by accusing but by forgiving. That is the wonder of holiness He now reveals to us. In the fire of wrath His compassion grows warm and tender. "I am God and not man," He declares, "the Holy One in your midst, and I will not come to destroy" (Hos. 11:9)!

After the purifying Lutheran education will delight in nothing more than to sing praises to our God and to "give thanks at the remembrance of His holiness" (Ps. 30:4 AV). We shall hallow God's name by teaching the Word of God clearly and purely and by living out the holiness God has invested in His people. To hallow God's name will be Lutheran education's entire philosophy, if it needs a philosophy. As we continue to search and grow in God's Word, we shall only amplify what His holiness really means. We shall discover how the name of God penetrates the hidden crevasses of life, reaching into secret places where we had never realized its potential. Even to begin the exploration of such possibilities would require another book. It does not belong to any one writer or even committee, however, to make the discoveries that reveal the splendor of God's name and glory. All pastors and teachers, and all the members of Christ's body are to share in that wonder. For "all the Lord's people [are] prophets," each in terms of his own gifts. The Lord has "put His spirit upon them" all (Num. 11:29). That is what conferences and books and classrooms are all about. That is what every free interchange of questions and searching is all about, wherever two or three are gathered together in the name of Christ and under the Word of God.

"Holy is his name," Mary sang (Luke 1:49), echoing the "Holy, holy, holy" of the seraphim in Isaiah's vision (Is. 6:3). We do not make His name holy. It is holy in itself. Our joy is only to discover what it means to let God be God and to rejoice in His holy name. For then we can be little children resting in His lap.[7] We can give up trying to guess His thoughts or to comprehend His ways.[8] He is our God, and we let Him finish His creation by molding and remolding us as He will.

Therefore we praise Him for His goodness. We trust His everlasting mercy even in trouble and suffering. We walk with Him humbly and without fear. We dare to lay before Him even our wrongness and sin, counting on His surprising promise that He can turn even these into good. Then we can rejoice to use the gifts He has given each of us without feeling superior or inferior to anyone. We can value the gifts of others and receive love without embarrassment. We can recognize the unity of the Spirit, and strive to keep it in the bond of peace.[9] We can love and forgive hurts without feeling hurt, and suffer wrong and oppression without anger or division. For we ourselves have become holy, different from what we once were. And in our own holiness we begin to manifest to one another and to our world little glimpses of the Lord's own holy surprises.

That's all there is! But that "all" is everything, and forever.

Footnotes for Epilogue

[1] On the material and formal principles, see Chapter IV, note 8.

[2] *A Short Explanation of Dr. Martin Luther's Small Catechism* (St. Louis: Concordia Publishing House, 1943), pp. 39-42.

[3] We have not attempted in this book to get at the issues of the Bible and science. The distinction we propose in Chapter IV seems essential for dealing with such questions. There would be no conflict of the sort we have experienced if we understood clearly what the "theological reality" of Scripture as the Word of God is, in distinction from its "historical reality." Conflicts arise only when the historical line is turned vertical, as though it too were "theological." As a result the church's energies and anxieties are consumed in battles which really have nothing to do with the Word of God and the cross of Christ. Exegetical matters then come to be regarded as matters of doctrine, and what is genuinely doctrine becomes mixed and blurred by opinions and speculations of men.

[4] The reference is again to the 62d of Luther's 95 Theses.

[5] Eph. 5:26-27.

[6] Is. 40:2.

[7] Ps. 131:2.

[8] Is. 55:8.

[9] Eph. 4:3.